A YOUNG READER'S EDITION OF
LAND OF HOPE

For Tunku,

Bill

WILFRED M. McCLAY

A YOUNG READER'S EDITION OF
LAND OF HOPE

An Invitation to the Great American Story

VOLUME ONE

Encounter
BOOKS

NEW YORK · LONDON

First American edition published in 2022 by Encounter Books, an activity of Encounter for Culture and Education, Inc., a nonprofit, tax-exempt corporation. Encounter Books website address: www.encounterbooks.com

Manufactured in the United States and printed on acid-free paper. The paper used in this publication meets the minimum requirements of ANSI-NISO Z39.48—1992 (R 1997) (*Permanence of Paper*).

Maps found on pages 34 and 193 are by David Lindroth.

FIRST AMERICAN EDITION

LIBRARY OF CONGRESS CATALOGING-IN-PUBLICATION DATA

Names: McClay, Wilfred M., author.
Title: Land of Hope: An Invitation to the Great American Story / Wilfred M. McClay. Other titles: A Young Reader's Edition of Land of Hope
Description: A Young Reader's Edition. | New York: Encounter Books, 2022. | Includes bibliographical references and index. |
Identifiers: LCCN 2021041707 (print) | LCCN 2021041708 (ebook) |
ISBN 9781641771702 (v.1; paperback) | ISBN 9781641772709 (v.2; paperback) |
ISBN 9781641771719 (v.1; ebook) | ISBN 9781641772716 (v.2; ebook)
Subjects: LCSH: United States—History—Juvenile literature.
Classification: LCC E178.3 .M143 2022 (print) | LCC E178.3 (ebook) |
DDC 973—dc23
LC record available at https://lccn.loc.gov/2021041707
LC ebook record available at https://lccn.loc.gov/2021041708

1 2 3 4 5 6 7 8 9 20 22

Cover image: Thomas Chambers, *Summer: Fishermen Netting* [detail], 1850s. Oil on canvas, 46.35 × 61.91 cm. Gift of Maxim Karolik for the M. and M. Karolik Collection of American Paintings, 1815–1865. 62.266. Photograph © [1850s] Museum of Fine Arts, Boston

Cover design by Carl W. Scarbrough

FOR JULIE
my bright and morning star
and favorite young reader

Every generation rewrites the past. In easy times history is more or less of an ornamental art, but in times of danger we are driven to the written record by a pressing need to find answers to the riddles of today. We need to know what kind of firm ground other men, belonging to generations before us, have found to stand on. In spite of changing conditions of life they were not very different from ourselves, their thoughts were the grandfathers of our thoughts, they managed to meet situations as difficult as those we have to face, to meet them sometimes lightheartedly, and in some measure to make their hopes prevail. We need to know how they did it.

In times of change and danger when there is a quicksand of fear under men's reasoning, a sense of continuity with generations gone before can stretch like a lifeline across the scary present and get us past that idiot delusion of the exceptional Now that blocks good thinking. That is why, in times like ours, when old institutions are caving in and being replaced by new institutions not necessarily in accord with most men's preconceived hopes, political thought has to look backwards as well as forwards.

JOHN DOS PASSOS
"The Use of the Past,"
from *The Ground We Stand On: Some Examples from the History of a Political Creed* (1941)

CONTENTS

PREFACE

THIS YOUNG READER'S EDITION of *Land of Hope* arose in response to popular demand, in the wake of *Land of Hope*'s gratifying success with older readers when it first appeared in May 2019. Many such readers – especially teachers and parents – expressed the wish for a book with *Land of Hope*'s balanced perspective on the American past that would also be more accessible to young students, especially those who are experiencing their first formal exposure to American history (usually around the fifth or sixth grade).

Their wish has been our command, and the book you have before you is the result. In writing the book, I have consistently sought to simplify and distill without ever dumbing down, and I hope I've been successful. I know that despite all my efforts, some passages, with their unfamiliar vocabulary or concepts, will challenge students. But learning to face and meet such challenges, and occasionally to look things up, is part of a superior education. My years of experience have convinced me that most students can meet and overcome any challenges this text presents. In addition, the goal here, as in *Land of Hope*, is something more than mastery of a subject. Ultimately, the book is meant to help in the formation of mature, informed, engaged, and grateful American citizens.

INTRODUCTION

WHY STUDY HISTORY? There have been many good answers to that question. One of the best was given thousands of years ago by the Roman statesman Cicero. This is what he said: "To be ignorant of what occurred before you were born is to remain always a child."

That's a pretty strong endorsement for the study of the past. And it doesn't apply only to our individual lives. When we choose to be ignorant about our past as a country, as a nation, as a people, we make a similar mistake. Every one of us, without exception, was born into a world that we didn't make, under conditions we didn't create. We became what we are, in part, because of those things that came before us and helped to shape us. Shouldn't we want to know about them?

Think about it on a personal level. Consider the story of your own life. The story didn't begin with you. You emerged in the middle of things, already part of a bigger and longer story. You didn't invent the words you speak, or the foods you eat, or the songs you sing. You didn't build the home you grew up in, or pave the streets you walked, or invent the subjects you learned in school.

Other people did those things before you. Other people prepared the way in advance of your coming. Other people, especially your parents, taught you to walk, to talk, to read, to dress, to behave properly, and everything else that goes with normal, everyday life in a civilized society. These are things that you mainly take for granted. But you shouldn't, if you are really going to understand who you are.

And that's not all. It's important to remember that the people who came before you didn't come into the world knowing these things either. The story didn't begin with them. They, too, came into a world they didn't make. Your parents didn't invent themselves any more than you did. They were children once too. They had to be taught. And the people who taught them were just the same in that regard, taught by people before them, who were taught by people before them, and by people before them, and so on, an ever-lengthening chain, reaching far back into the past.

We carry that past forward into the present much more than we realize. We do it every single day. Even at the moment of birth, we are already in the middle of things, carrying forward a whole history of our parents and their families and all the others who came before.

So how far back should you go in telling your own story? You could go back pretty far if you wanted. Many people are fascinated by tracing out their family history, their genealogy. But too much of that gets in the way of the most important part of the story. Too much detail complicates the picture and defeats the ultimate purpose.

What we call history is the same way. It is not the whole past in every little detail. It doesn't include everything, and it couldn't. That would be overwhelming. Imagine if a historical account of a great event were written to include everything that could be known about that moment in time – every bird in the sky, every leaf in the wind, every car on the street, every thought in the mind of every participant.

We can't make sense of things that way, when there is too much information coming at us all at once. Instead, a proper history is a careful selection out of the past, like a carefully trimmed photograph. It is organized wisely and truthfully, in a way that allows us to see the larger pattern of the past and to focus on the details of a particular story.

The story that this book seeks to tell, the Great American Story, is exactly like this. It is not the story of everything. It can't be. It will have to leave many things out. But it's a story about who we are and about the stream of time we share. It aims to give us a clearer understanding of the "middle of things" in which we already find ourselves.

In addition, it has been written with a particular purpose in mind. It is designed to help us learn, above all else, the things we must know to become informed, self-aware, and dedicated citizens of the United States of America. That knowledge includes a knowledge of our history. Becoming a good citizen is about more than just knowing the laws. It means acquiring a sense of membership, of belonging – of claiming the nation's past as your own. We hope it helps you to understand and appreciate the country in whose midst you find yourself and makes you more capable of carrying out the duties of citizens, including the preservation of what is best in our nation's institutions and ideals. The goal, in short, is to help us be appreciative and responsible members of the society of which we are already a part – to live, as Cicero might put it, as wise and knowledgeable adults.

So let's begin.

1 · BEGINNINGS

BUT WHERE TO BEGIN? How far back do we go?

If we try to tell the whole story, we might end up going back many thousands of years. And there's much we really don't know for certain. We believe that the first human settlers came over into the western hemisphere perhaps 20,000–30,000 years ago from northeastern Asia, probably by crossing over what is now the Bering Strait, the frigid waters that separate Russia and Alaska. From there, we believe that these first immigrants to America gradually filtered outward and downward, eventually populating all of North and South America.

From those migrant peoples emerged some highly advanced cultures, which rose, flourished, and fell. The Mayas and Aztecs of Mexico, the Incas of Peru, the North American settlements, the Pueblo of the Southwest – all of them blazed a trail across time but left behind for us only a few physical reminders of themselves, silent clues to a vanished way of life.

There is something haunting about these remaining traces of earlier civilizations. In a sense, they are a part of our history, even if we know next to nothing about them. Their mysterious life and death haunt us with a somber recognition: the realization that our civilization, too, is perishable and can disappear in the same way.

But we won't begin our story with those civilizations past, for the simple reason that they had no direct or significant role in the establishment of the settlements and institutions that would eventually make up the country we know as the United States.

Neither did the later discovery and exploration around the year

1000 of a New World by adventurous Norse seamen, such as Leif Eriksson of Iceland. He tried to plant a colony in what is now the large Canadian island of Newfoundland. He and other Norsemen tried their best to establish a settlement in this chilly newfound land to the west. But their efforts came to nothing and are generally counted as historical curiosities. They are interesting false starts on American history, perhaps, but no more than that.

And yet, on further reflection, I need to modify that statement, for the lost civilizations of the first Americans and the episodic voyages of Eriksson and other Norsemen point toward the deepest sources of American history. They point to the presence of America in the world's imagination as an idea, as a land of hope, of refuge and opportunity, of a second chance at life for those willing to take it. Ideas are as much a part of history as battles, elections, and other deeds. And that idea, and the persistence of that idea, is one of the themes of this book. It is in the book's title itself.

Perhaps I am making a stretch here. After all, how can we ever know for sure what led those earliest peoples 20,000 years ago to cross over into Alaska and make the cold, dangerous journey to populate a new continent? How can we know what was in their minds? Were they pushed by war or scarcity? Were they hunters who were following their prey? Or were they pulled there by the sense of promise, opportunity, or adventure that those lands offered?

We don't know. The answers to these questions will probably always remain beyond our reach. But we know that the Norsemen's brave impulse of over a thousand years ago, which drove them to go forth in search of new lands, came out of something more than necessity. They were drawn to cross the icy and turbulent waters of the North Atlantic by the lure of available western lands and by a restless desire to explore and settle them. They were being influenced by ideas and sentiments that were already widespread in their time – a thousand years after Christ and five hundred years before Christopher Columbus.

From as far back as we know, there was always a fascination with the West, the land of the setting sun. Leif's explorer father, Erik the Red, was playing on that very fascination when he gave the alluring name of "Greenland" to the largely frozen island we know by that name today. He was appealing to an idea already long embedded in literature, myth, and religion. The idea? That new lands of plenty and wonder and mystery were out there – perhaps even an earthly paradise – waiting to be found, lying somewhere in lands beyond the western horizon.

This message was especially appealing at the dawn of the new millennium, at a time when Europe was still struggling to get back on its feet after the collapse of the Roman Empire. But the message itself was not new. The ancient Greeks had spoken this way, a millennium and a half earlier. They sang of the Isles of the Blessed, where the heroes and gods of their mythology dwelled in a fertile land where there was no winter. They sang of the Elysian Fields, which the poet Homer located on the western edge of the earth, beside the stream of the world's seas.

Centuries later, at the outset of a modern age of exploration, Sir Thomas More's book *Utopia* (1516) described an ideal society located on an island in the West, as did Francis Bacon's *The New Atlantis* (1627), whose very title recalled one of the most enduring legends of the West – the strange story of the isle of Atlantis, a fully developed past civilization with kings of great and mighty power that had been swallowed up by the seas and disappeared forever from view.

So the West had already been thought of, in Europe, as a symbol for renewal and discovery, a place of wealth and plenty, a land of hope – an anticipation of what a New World could be like.

So, since we must begin in the middle of things, we'll start our history of America in the middle of Europe's history. In fact, the two histories cannot be understood apart from one another. America is best understood as an offshoot of Europe; even the name "America" comes from the first name of the Italian-born navigator and explorer Amerigo Vespucci, who was among the first to speculate that the lands Columbus discovered were not part of Asia but part of an entirely new landmass.

But America would prove to be an unusual kind of offshoot. It was not like a new branch emerging out of the trunk of a great tree. Nor was it a careful and deliberate transplant, a copy of what had already been established in Europe. Instead, it would draw upon certain parts of Europe, particularly English laws and customs, fragments that had been broken off from the whole and would give those fragments a new home, in a new land where they could develop and flourish in ways that would never have been possible in their native land. But there was nothing systematic about it. So much of it was unpredictable, unplanned, unanticipated. The writer Lewis Mumford memorably expressed this surprising process in a single brilliant sentence: "The settlement of America had its origins in the unsettlement of Europe."

What did Mumford mean by this? He meant that by the time of Christopher Columbus's famous voyage in 1492, which was one of the main events in the making of America, Europe was becoming a dramatically different place from what it had been for the three preceding centuries, during the relatively stable and orderly years we now call the High Middle Ages (1000–1300). But by the Late Middle Ages (1300–1500), Europe was entering the modern age. It was no longer stable. Instead, it was becoming a place of widespread change, innovation, and disruption – in technology, in political and social practices, in economics, in religion.

If any one of these innovations or disruptions had come along just by itself, without the company of others – say, if the desire for an expansion of global commerce had not been accompanied by powerful new navigational instruments that made such commerce possible – its effects would have been far less pronounced. But by coming all together at once, these changes gathered strength from one another, so that they contributed to a more general transforming fire, as when many small blazes combine to fuel a large blaze.

This is what happens in all great historical transformations.

They arise not out of a single cause but out of the coming together of a large number of causes. This unsettling transformation of Europe that was already well under way in 1492 was throwing off flames that would land in other places and set off transformations there as well. The exploration and settlement of America would be one of the most consequential of these. It was, just as Mumford said, the product of a host of great European disruptions: economic, social, religious, technological, and cultural.

What makes the story even more surprising is the fact that the movement toward the West actually began with a movement toward the East. Some key changes for Europe were caused unintentionally by the Crusades. These were a Church-sanctioned military effort in the eleventh, twelfth, and thirteenth centuries to free the Holy Lands from their Muslim occupiers, who had in the four centuries since the death of Mohammed in 632 conquered two-thirds of the Christian world. We often misunderstand the Crusades today. Far from being intended as an early act in the unsettlement of medieval Europe, or an act of unprovoked aggression, the Crusades were meant to be part of Europe's ongoing work of restoring what it had lost in the years since the fall of Rome. The Crusades were in many ways a perfect expression of the high medieval spirit in Western Europe, a world that was dominated by the Roman Catholic Church as both a spiritual and political (and military) power.

But we are concerned in this book with one of the indirect effects of the Crusades. Because they were fought in the East, they brought Europeans into contact with the riches of the lands along the eastern shores of the Mediterranean Sea. This led to an opening up of overland trade routes to Asia, from which many desirable goods, such as rugs, silks, gold brocade, perfumes, teas, precious stones, dyewoods, and unusual spices like pepper, nutmeg, and cloves could be imported.

Small wonder that the East came to hold such a fascination for many Europeans. A widely read memoir by the Venetian traveler

Marco Polo, featuring spellbinding stories of his exploits along the Silk Road and in the lavish court of the Mongol emperor Kublai Khan, gave Europeans their first direct knowledge of the fabled wealth of China and Central Asia. *The Travels of Marco Polo* influenced the imaginations of future explorers like Columbus and Ferdinand Magellan. The benefits of commerce with Asian cultures were obvious and enticing, and so was the adventure of it all.

There were many obstacles, however. Overland trade with the East along the legendary Silk Road was slow and dangerous, and became more so after the fall of Constantinople to the Ottoman Turks in 1453. It could take a year to go from Venice to Beijing by land, crossing mountains and deserts on narrow trails with cargoes packed on the backs of horses and camels. Turks and other unfriendly groups controlled the land routes to the east, so that even if travelers were able to elude bandits, they would have to pay local rulers and middlemen along the way. This made the goods very expensive by the time they finally arrived at markets in Europe. As consumer demand for these luxuries grew and interest in trade with the East swelled, finding a better way of getting there and back became more and more desirable. The search was on to discover an all-water route to the East, which, if found, would go a long way toward solving these problems.

This search boosted attention to oceangoing exploration and stimulated a passion for extending and mapping the boundaries of the known world. Fortunately, vital technological inventions and improvements in navigation and ship design were becoming available, and these made such expansive voyages possible. Advances in mapmaking and astronomical navigation; invention of the dry magnetic compass, the astrolabe, the quadrant, the cross-staff, and other such instruments; and the development of new ships, such as the oceangoing Genoese *carrack* and the fast and maneuverable Portuguese *caravel* – all of these changed the game entirely when it came to seaboard exploration.

The innovations did not stop there, though. The rapid expansion of trade was remaking the social and political map of Europe at the same time that explorers were redrawing the physical map. In earlier eras, wealth and power had rested in the hands of those who owned land. This was a system called *feudalism*, in which the common people served the nobles in exchange for their protection and the use of their land. But that was about to change. With the expansion of seaborne trade came a rise in the economic and political power of a merchant class, made up of those traders who had become wealthy from the risks and rewards of expanding commerce. As their wealth grew, so did the importance of the bustling market towns and port cities where the merchants' commercial activities would be concentrated, places where a host of related middle-class businesspersons and professionals – bankers, lawyers, insurance providers, outfitters and suppliers of goods and services, teachers – would set up shop and thrive.

These changes would have far-reaching effects, further unsettling the existing order. As the power of the new merchant class grew, that meant a corresponding decline in the power of old local and regional aristocracies, whose power had been based on their possession of land in a feudal economy. As one class was rising, the other class was falling. The static older ways would be no competition for the dynamic, wealth-generating, and disruptive new economics of trade.

Such changes would give rise in turn to new political structures. In Italy, ambitious merchant-princes used their new wealth to create powerful city-states, such as Florence and Venice. Such cities featured glamorous palaces, churches, and other architectural and artistic wonders echoing the glories of Greek and Roman antiquity. In other parts of Europe, the changes would lead to the emergence of great national monarchies – unified and centralized kingdoms over which individual rulers would be able to govern with vast authority and power. Such monarchs managed to break the hold of the local nobles and regional aristocrats who had dominated the feudal system through their control of so much land. The new monarchs were able to create a unified nation featuring a new kind of national-scale order – something not seen since the fall of the

Roman Empire, over a thousand years before! A strong and unified nation meant a uniform national currency, a removal of barriers to trade, and a professional standing military force that kept internal order and supported the nation's interests abroad. All these innovations would further the interests of the merchant and middle classes, even as they helped to build the nation.

By 1492, four such national states were evolving in Europe: France, England, Spain, and Portugal. All four had both the wealth and the motivation to support the further exploration that would be needed to find a water route to the East and to expand the reach of their commerce and growing power.

It would be Portugal, though, that took the initiative in this Age of Discovery, early in the fifteenth century, under the guidance of a man known as Prince Henry the Navigator. Portugal was a small country. But as the westernmost country of mainland Europe, with an extensive Atlantic coastline and magnificent ports like Lisbon and Oporto, it was perfectly situated to be an oceangoing power.

In fact, Portugal would become the first global empire in the history of the world. Under Henry's leadership, it became a magnet for the best navigators and seamen from all over Europe, drawn to take part in the expeditions he sponsored. Skilled Portuguese crews combed the entire west coast of Africa, opening it up to commerce. Eventually, explorers like Bartholomew Dias and Vasco da Gama would round the southern end of the African continent and, by 1498, establish the long-sought waterborne path to India.

The example of such Portuguese exploits drew Christopher Columbus away from his native Italian city-state of Genoa to settle in Lisbon at the age of twenty-six. Though still relatively young, Columbus was already a highly experienced and capable sailor who had been to ports in the Mediterranean and northern Europe. In partnership with his brother, he made voyages under the Portuguese flag as far north as the Arctic Ocean, south along the coasts of West Africa, and west to the Azore Islands.

And he was very ambitious. Like everyone else of the time, he was obsessed with the idea of discovering an all-water route to "the Indies," as the Far East was called. But he had his own ideas about the best way of doing it. Everyone else was confident that going east and rounding Africa was the key; Bartholomew Dias seemed to have confirmed that when he rounded Africa in 1488. But Columbus became convinced that going west would be both faster and more direct. He formulated a plan for an expedition that would prove it.

(By the way, just so you know, he did *not* undertake his voyage to prove that the Earth was round. That's a common conception, but it's entirely wrong. In fact, everyone in Columbus's time knew that the earth was round. The ancient Greek philosopher Aristotle even claimed to have proven it, nearly two thousand years before Columbus. People still had a great deal of disagreement, though, about the *size* of the earth.)

When he took his plan to the king of Portugal in search of financial support, however, Columbus was turned down, twice. He appealed to leaders in Genoa and Venice, in England, and then in Spain but had no luck with any of them. All of them said the plan was impractical and that it grossly underestimated the distances involved. What if the earth was much bigger than Columbus imagined?

Finally, however, after determined negotiations, Columbus was able to persuade the Spanish monarchs Ferdinand and Isabella to support him. On August 3, 1492, he set sail from Palos de la Frontera in Spain aboard a large *carrack* called the *Santa Maria*, accompanied by two *caravels*. He was carrying a Latin passport and a sheaf of letters of introduction, including a letter of introduction from Ferdinand and Isabella to the Emperor of China, just in case. He also brought along a Jewish scholar who was fluent in Arabic, so that he would be able to communicate with any Muslims he encountered at his Asian destinations. What may have been lacking in hard evidence for Columbus's theories he more than made up for by the fervency of his commitment. He fully expected that he would be ending up in the Far East.

On October 12, his party spotted land, one of the islands of the Bahamas. Columbus named the island "San Salvador," meaning "Holy Savior." What they had found was in fact an outpost of a new and unexplored landmass. But Columbus refused to believe that these lands could be anything other than the "Indies" he had counted upon finding, and he accordingly called the gentle Arawak natives who greeted them by the name "Indians."

But something wasn't quite right. He found none of the plentiful spices and jewels, gold and silver, and other precious goods that Marco Polo's account had led him to expect. The Caribbean islands were very beautiful, but they were full of exotic plants and trees that did not correspond to anything he knew about or had read about. He was able to admit that he did not recognize them. But he was not able to imagine that he was looking at an entirely New World.

Between 1492 and 1503, Columbus commanded four round-trip voyages between Spain and the Americas, all sponsored by the Spanish Crown. He was not the first European to reach the Americas, but he was the first to establish enduring contact between the Old World and the New. Hence his voyages are of great significance in the history of Europe, and they also mark a proper beginning for our story. They mark the first elements of Europe's unsettlement that would reach western shores and begin to give rise to the permanent settlement of America.

But Columbus was not able to see it that way. He insisted, in the face of all evidence to the contrary, that the lands he visited during those voyages were part of Asia. He was possessed by an iron determination that his initial theory *had* to be true. By his third voyage, which took him to present-day Venezuela, he came to believe that, while that land was not the Indies proper, it was merely a barrier between him and them, and all that remained was to find a strait or other passage through.

His final voyage was an unsuccessful effort to find that strait, a journey that took him even to what would much later be the site of the Panama Canal, just a few miles away from the immensity of a Pacific Ocean that he never knew was there, never knew existed.

So close! But he returned home in disgrace and was regarded as a failure.

What a strange irony it is. He had made one of the most important discoveries in human history. And yet he didn't quite realize it. He was never able to understand what he had discovered. He was obsessed with finding a new way to reach the riches of the East. But that obsession was the force that had propelled him into a far more momentous discovery in the West, that mysterious land of mythic renewal. And yet he could not see what was before him with fresh and open eyes.

In 1951, almost five hundred years later, the American poet Robert Frost would capture this irony in a witty poem about Columbus called "And All We Call American." Here is a portion of that poem:

> *Had but Columbus known enough*
> *He might have boldly made the bluff*
> *That better than Da Gama's gold*
> *He had been given to behold*
> *The race's future trial place,*
> *A fresh start for the human race.*
> *America is hard to see.*
> *Less partial witnesses than he*
> *In book on book have testified*
> *They could not see it from outside –*
> *Or inside either for that matter.*

America is hard to see. Columbus had trouble seeing America for the new thing that it was, and would be. He was not the first, and he would not be the last. Read on, and you'll see.

2 · UNSETTLED EUROPE

LET'S CAST OUR EYES back a few centuries to the year 1300, when the civilization of Western Europe in the Middle Ages was reaching its peak. That world was tightly unified around the Roman Catholic faith, and the Church's power and authority could be seen everywhere. Kings were crowned by clergymen, and every major town had a magnificent cathedral at its center, visible proof of the people's faithfulness. The Pope was a powerful political and religious figure, and the world's leading thinkers were church theologians. It was the high tide of Christendom, of Christianity as both a worldly and spiritual power.

That high tide didn't last. High tides never do. It would experience a series of rude disruptions: death-dealing plagues, fierce church quarrels, and growing feelings of nationalism. All of these things together contributed to the great upheaval of the Protestant Reformation, which shattered the religious unity of Europe forever.

The Church's prosperity and power were a big part of its problem. Peasants and poor laborers resented the Church's grand displays of wealth. Middle-class businessmen wanted to be free of the Church's interference in the economy. Kings and princes wanted to be masters of their own territories. And religious reformers were increasingly convinced that the Church was guilty of terrible errors in its teaching. The stage was set for an eruption.

The first large outburst came in 1517 from the German monk Martin Luther, a pious and passionate man who took offense at the Church's practice of selling indulgences, a purchase that was thought to ease the path through the afterlife for one's dead relatives. But

Luther's objections went much deeper than that. They went to the very heart of Christianity's self-understanding as a religion of redemption and salvation.

Luther wondered how any person could be deserving of heaven when all of us are so very flawed and sinful. What could possibly "justify" us in God's eyes? What can make us right with God and save us from damnation? Was it a lifetime of consistently good "works"? No, Luther insisted, that couldn't work. No one can be good enough to "earn" salvation. Only their faith in Jesus Christ, granted to them by God through an act of divine grace, could secure their salvation. This was not something that could be bestowed on them by a priest, or by the institution of the Church, or by any external actions whatsoever. No, it had to be a direct encounter between the soul of the individual believer and God.

This idea of "justification by faith" was radically unsettling. The Catholic understanding of the priesthood had insisted that the priest stood in the middle between individual believers and God. But if Luther was right, that meant that the Church had been wrong. And Luther went even further, arguing that a great deal of the theology and structure of the Church, including the authority of the Pope, had been invented without reference to the Bible – a grave error, in his view, because only the words of the Bible, he insisted, had final authority in matters of Christian faith.

Despite the challenge represented by these assertions, Luther did not set out to produce a split in the Catholic Church. Nor was he at all interested in causing political or social revolution. But the forces he had set into motion could not easily be stopped or slowed. Like a snowball rolling down a mountain slope, they gradually became transformed into an avalanche of change.

The other great religious reformer of the time, John Calvin, had an outlook that resembled Luther's in many respects but differed in several important ways. Calvin strongly emphasized the idea of predestination, arguing that God's infinite knowledge and power meant that He must have already decided who would be saved – the elect – and who would be damned. You might think that a doctrine like this would make Calvinists lazy and contented and cause them just to wait around for the inevitable to happen. But the opposite was the case. Calvinists were full of passionate conviction and wanted to reform the world. They especially wanted to purify the Church by restoring it to something simpler, closer to what they thought it had been in the time of Jesus. In Scotland and England, and then later in America, these zealous, reform-minded Calvinists would become known as Puritans.

Now we must turn our attention to England, where the Reformation unfolded in a unique way. At the time that the Reformation was happening in Germany, King Henry VIII of England (1509–47) was among the fiercest defenders of the Catholic Church. But Henry was also a king, and he wanted to have a male heir to inherit his throne. Unfortunately, his first wife, Catherine of Aragon, had not been able to give him a son in twenty-three years of marriage. But when he asked Pope Clement VII to grant him an annulment, which would dissolve his marriage to Catherine and free him to remarry, the Pope said no.

Henry reacted with fury. He separated the Church of England from the Roman Catholic Church; made himself its Supreme Head and replaced the Archbishop of Canterbury with someone he chose, who then granted his annulment; and married him to young Anne Boleyn. Henry seized church lands, which he then handed out to his followers as a way of securing their loyalty. In the blink of an eye, he had decisively stripped the Roman Catholic Church of all meaningful power in England.

Thus the Reformation that Henry started in England was the near opposite of Luther's. It came about for political reasons rather than religious ones. Hence many of the important religious questions were left undecided, and the Church of England would go on to have strong divisions between its inherited Catholic traditions and its determined Protestant reformers, particularly those influenced by Calvinism. These divisions would be vitally important to the shape that American religion would take a century or more later.

In religion, as in a multitude of other ways too, the English influence in the settling of North America turned out to be far greater than that of any other country or culture.

But there was nothing inevitable about its turning out that way. In fact, the Spanish were overwhelmingly dominant in the western hemisphere for more than a hundred years after Columbus's voyages of discovery, a time span including nearly all the 1500s. During those years, the Spanish rose to their greatest heights. Their arts and literature flourished, and they enjoyed a free hand in exploring and exploiting the resources of the New World. Exploit them they did. Beginning with Columbus's ventures in the Caribbean, and then the explorations of Vasco Núñez de Balboa, Ferdinand Magellan, Hernando Cortés, and others, a bold group of explorers working for Spain would establish a Spanish presence and a distinctively Spanish pattern of settlement in the New World. They would make the Spanish Empire into the most powerful in the world.

The motives behind Spain's push into the New World were mixed. There was religious passion behind the efforts of Catholic missionaries, men and women whose desire to serve God was so great that they were willing to endure extreme hardships and suffer martyrdom. But there was also a strong element of materialism driving the colonization effort, a readiness to plunder the land for its gold and silver and other riches, without regard for the needs or wishes of the native populations.

In addition, the Spanish government tried to control their colonies as much as possible. They wanted to make them as profitable as possible for the mother country. Colonization for the Spanish was an entirely centralized undertaking, serving the purposes of the Spanish Crown and leaving little if any room for the colonists to run their own affairs and do as they pleased. There was simply no thought of developing free commerce with the native populations or, more generally, of enabling those colonies to mature into free and self-governing societies.

The Spanish dominance over the New World didn't go unchallenged. Spain's many rivals saw to that. Beginning in the 1520s, French privateers – private vessels that had been allowed to operate as warships – started raiding Spanish treasure ships returning from the colonies with their precious cargoes. By the mid-1500s, the Dutch and the English were also supporting privateers of their own, such as those under the command of the colorful "seadogs" John Hawkins and Francis Drake. Eventually, the Spanish ruler Philip II decided he'd had enough of English harassment. He would seek a large-scale military showdown with England. He was confident he could crush her ambitions once and for all, overthrow the rule of Queen Elizabeth I, and restore Catholicism as England's official state religion.

In 1588, Philip assembled an "Invincible Armada" of 130 ships, the largest such fleet ever seen in Europe to date, which was to escort an army of some 55,000 men who would invade England. At least that was the plan, and given these large numbers, the battle could have been highly one-sided. But the English fleet had superior tactics and more maneuverable vessels, while the Spanish fleet was led by a well-connected aristocrat who had no experience as a naval commander. The slow-moving Armada was harassed at every turn by nimble English attackers, who even used a night attack by unmanned fireships loaded with gunpowder to create confusion and panic among the Spanish. And the English had something else working in their favor: an unexpected storm (it was called a "Protestant wind") that swept much of the Spanish fleet out into the North Sea.

The English also had an inspirational leader in Queen Elizabeth, who rode out in her ceremonial armor to address militia troops at West Tilbury, poised to defend against the Spanish invaders. "Let tyrants fear," she declared;

I have always so behaved myself, that under God I have placed my chiefest strength and safeguard in the loyal hearts and goodwill of my subjects; and, therefore, I am come amongst you as you see at this time, not for my recreation and disport, but being resolved, in the midst and heat of battle, to live or die amongst you all – to lay down for my God, and for my kingdoms, and for my people, my honour and my blood even in the dust.

Henry VIII may not have gotten an adult son to be the successor he had so badly wanted. But England got something even better in his brilliant, valiant, and thoroughly exceptional daughter.

The English were able to defeat the Armada decisively. In doing so, they accomplished far more than merely averting a Spanish invasion. They changed the balance of power in Europe irreversibly. From 1588 on, the star of England was on the rise, and the star of Spain was in decline.

The defeat of the Armada is important to American history, because it had an enormous effect on the kind of culture that North America would come to have – and the kind of culture it would *not* have. That is not to say that North America would ever be exclusively English and that all traces of Spanish heritage and influence would disappear from it overnight. Far from it. All you have to do is notice the many Spanish place-names – Los Angeles, Santa Fe, San Antonio – that persisted across the continent to see that this did not happen. But the defeat of the Armada opened the way for England to take the lead in settling North America. The result would be a continent and nation whose institutions and laws and government would draw deeply on English roots. Let's find out more about what those roots were.

3 · ENGLISH EXPERIMENTS

WHY DID ENGLISH DOMINANCE turn out to be so important? How did it affect the shape that English colonies would take? Part of the answer has to do with England being an island nation. That meant it was cut off and was able to develop in relative isolation from other peoples and cultures. That meant it would be able to create institutions and customs that were very special and very different from what was going on at the same time on the European continent.

What was going on in those other countries? The monarchies of early modern France and Spain were embracing *absolutism*, a term that means greater and greater centralization of power in the hands of a single ruler – a ruler who was thought to rule by God-given right. But the English followed a very different path. They created a system in which the power of rulers was limited by opposing forces that divided and restrained their power. The king had to share his power with aristocrats and wealthy landowners. They met independently in a legislative body called the Parliament that, among other things, held the "power of the purse," the ability to authorize taxes and control the Crown's access to them. Also, the Crown could not control government on the local level. That was handled by counties and towns, each of which had its own roster of local public officials – justices of the peace, sheriffs, magistrates, and the like.

Most important of all, the Crown's power was limited by the English belief that the people possessed certain fundamental rights that no monarch could take away. Such rights were grounded in something more permanent than the wishes of rulers. They were seated deep in the English tradition of *common law*, an approach to the law that relied on the decision of previous courts – what are called "precedents" – built up over many years by many generations of judges. The common law was a reflection of the customs of the people. Rights such as the right to trial by jury or protection from unwarranted search and seizure were held sacred because they were protected by both law and custom. They were part of the English way of life.

Another important difference was in the English approach to colonization. Unlike the Spanish, the English generally sought to transplant an English way of life to their settlements. But the English approach was also far less controlled. In fact, it was downright freewheeling, in ways that reflected an English fondness for creativity and commerce. English colonization of the New World was never a centrally directed government project. The Crown was, of course, involved in various important ways. It was the Crown that granted licenses to colonize "Virginia," as the whole area of North America claimed by England was then known. But in the end, English colonization was not directed by the government. It was largely a private undertaking.

Or rather, it was a collection of private undertakings, taken on by a diverse group of adventurers and visionaries. These efforts were not being coordinated with one another. Each one was seeking the fresh opportunities of the New World for its own purposes. Each was given an extraordinary degree of freedom in pursuing those ends without being steered by a larger national vision.

Each of these undertakings had its own profile, its own goals, its own way of understanding America as a land of hope. Hence the contrasts among them could be very striking, and very instructive. Perhaps the sharpest contrast of all came at the very beginning, between the colonies of Virginia and New England. It is a contrast worth exploring in some detail.

Virginia came first. The first permanent English colony would be established in 1607 at Jamestown, named for James I, Elizabeth's successor. The first to arrive there were some 105 men sent by the Virginia Company, a private company. Their goal? They were in search of wealth. In fact, their charter from the king could not have been clearer about it: they were empowered "to dig, mine, and search for all Manner of Mines of Gold, Silver, and Copper." They came to America to get rich.

Unfortunately, nearly all of them had been town dwellers in England, and they didn't have the skills to be pioneers. Few of them knew anything about building, farming, hunting, woodlore, and the like. The more well-off among them thought they were above most forms of manual labor. And since they were employees of the Virginia Company, they couldn't own their own property. That meant that they had little incentive to work hard and build up the colony, since so little of that additional wealth would end up in their pockets. The colony's future was on a collision course with the basic facts of human nature.

The whole arrangement would have been comic, if it weren't that the results were so bitterly tragic. More than half the settlers died during the first winter. Even more of them would have died had it not been for the generous gifts of food made to them by the Powhatan Indians in those early days.

But the colony managed to survive, saved from ruin by the heroic leadership of Captain John Smith, a strong-willed soldier-adventurer who took matters in hand. He imposed military-style discipline on the colonists, declared that only those who worked would be allowed to eat, put down rebellions and mutinies, and established a measure of peace and harmony – but only temporarily. Things seemed always on the edge of breakdown. There were no women or families in the colony, which strengthened the sense of impermanence, since groupings of unattached males did not build families or create the kind of stable institutions that are needed for civilized living. As of 1624, despite in-migration of more than fourteen thousand souls since 1607, the population of Jamestown stood at barely a thousand. In that year, the Virginia Company was dissolved, and Virginia became a royal colony.

By then, though, changes were afoot that would lead to stability. For one thing, the institution of private property had finally been established so that men who had come over as servants could now be landowners, a change that meant, as John Smith said, that the lazy man who used to "slip from his labour or slumber over his taske" now worked harder in a day than he used to work in a week.

But something else came along that finally saved the colony from certain collapse. It was the discovery of tobacco. Now, James I was no fan of tobacco. He called it a "filthy novelty" whose "black stinking fume" resembled "the horrible Stygian smoke of the pit that is bottomless" – that is to say, the pit of hell. But the rest of Europe didn't agree. Tobacco became a cash crop whose export to the home country and the rest of Europe was highly profitable. Over the rest of the seventeenth century, Virginia's tobacco production soared and provided a solid basis for general prosperity. With prosperity came more orderly political institutions, including a governor and legislative assembly, as well as the construction of roads and other internal improvements and the establishment of the Anglican Church. Virginia was on its way.

By this time, the colonies of New England had emerged, beginning with Plymouth Plantation in 1620 and then Massachusetts Bay in 1630, and they were very different from Virginia. If the earliest settlers of Virginia had been motivated primarily by material considerations, the New Englanders were driven almost entirely by religious zeal. Most of them were Puritans, men and women who believed the Church of England had not gone far enough to purge itself of what they considered to be its corruptions and who despaired of such a cleansing renewal ever taking place in their lifetimes. Best to go elsewhere and start over.

Most of them were comfortably middle class, which means that they were not pushed into taking this perilous voyage by poverty. Instead, they were willing to leave all their comforts behind and risk a fresh new start for the life of the Christian church – to be a New Zion in a new land. They understood themselves as on a divinely ordained mission, an "errand into the wilderness" in which they would seek to create "holy commonwealths," models for the reformation of the Church they left behind.

There were important differences between the first two New England colonies. The Plymouth colonists, a group sometimes called "the Pilgrims," were a small group of Separatists, which meant that they had abandoned the Church of England altogether as a hopelessly ruined body. They preferred to worship in independent congregational (i.e., self-governing) churches. After eleven years of living in exile in the Netherlands, they received permission from the Virginia Company to establish an English colony where they could practice their faith freely. Across the ocean they came in the battered old *Mayflower* and made landfall at what is today Cape Cod – which, unfortunately for them, was outside of the Virginia Company's authority and, indeed, outside the reach of any known government.

The group's leaders knew that this was a potentially dangerous situation. They worried that the colony might not be able to hold together in the absence of a larger controlling authority. In response to this peril, they drafted and signed a short document that would come to be called the "Mayflower Compact." In that document, they organized themselves as a political body and committed all those who signed the document to obey the laws and authorities.

It was an important milestone in the development of self-governing political institutions, and it followed the same pattern by which the New Englanders were organizing their religious life. In the Congregational churches, ordinary believers came together to form their own churches. Likewise, in the Mayflower Compact, a group of ordinary people came together to form their own government. It was an astonishing moment in history because it amounted to a real-world version of the theory that civil society could be created by an agreement among its individual members: what became known as a "social contract." This was a powerful idea, one that would go on to influence the Founders of the United States a century and a half later, when they sought to justify a revolution against Great Britain.

The Massachusetts Bay colony came ten years later. It would be much larger and better organized and would in the long run have far more influence over the eventual shape of colonial New England. The Massachusetts Bay Company, a group of Puritans led by the wealthy lawyer John Winthrop, received a charter from King Charles I, James's son. Winthrop and his group were Nonseparating Congregationalists, meaning that, unlike the Pilgrims, they had not separated, had not yet given up entirely on the Church of England. Nevertheless, in 1630, they undertook the voyage to America with a flotilla of seven ships, led by the *Arbella*, aboard which was Winthrop and the charter, which he had brought along with him rather than leaving it in England.

Before landing in America, Winthrop delivered a lay sermon aboard ship called "A Modell of Christian Charity," in which he reminded everyone on board of the settlement's mission and guiding purposes. The speech leaves one in no doubt about the fundamentally religious intentions behind the colony's existence and the hope that the godly community they were creating could eventually serve as a means of renewal for the Old World they had left behind. Said Winthrop, "We are entered into Covenant with [God] for this work.... For this end, we must be knit together, in this work, as one man.... We must delight in each other; make other's conditions our own; rejoice together, mourn together, labor and suffer together, always having before our eyes our commission and community in the work, as members of the same body.... We must consider that we shall be as a city upon a hill. The eyes of all people are upon us."

Let's pause for a moment and consider how audacious a statement this was, under the circumstances. Here they were, countless miles away from anyone or anything that was familiar to them. They had just crossed a vast ocean, were now cut off from the known world, and found themselves looking out at the edges of a wild and unfriendly wasteland. They were not reckless adventurers or roving pirates. They were middle-class families from comfortable homes who had chosen to throw all that away for the sake of their faith.

And now? How could they possibly imagine that the eyes of all people were upon them? They might as well have been landing on the surface of the moon. No one was watching, no one in the civilized world could know what they were doing. Surely there must have been some among them who trembled a bit, silently and inwardly, and wondered for a moment if it had not all been an act of madness that carried them so far away from all they had known, into the terrors and uncertainties of a strange and forbidding land.

Some of the desolation they must have been feeling was well expressed by William Bradford, who led the Pilgrim settlers when they arrived at Cape Cod ten years before:

> Being now passed the vast ocean, and a sea of troubles before them in expectations, they had now no friends to welcome them, nor inns to entertain or refresh their weatherbeaten bodies, no houses, or much less towns, to repair to, to seek for succor.... Besides, what could they see but a hideous and desolate wilderness, full of wild beasts and wild men? and what multitude of them there were, they knew not: for which way soever they turned their eyes (save upward to Heaven) they could have but little solace or content in respect of any outward object; for summer being ended, all things stand in appearance with a weatherbeaten face, and the whole country, full of woods and thickets, represented a wild and savage hew.
>
> If they looked behind them, there was a mighty ocean which they had passed, and was now as a main bar or gulf to separate them from all the civil parts of the world.... What could now sustain them but the spirit of God and his grace?

What, indeed, but their religious faith could have sustained them, just as it had drawn them across the seas? John Winthrop's words aboard the *Arbella* could not have been more true in that regard.

They do not betray any shred of doubt. The point of calling the colony-to-be a city upon a hill, an image that came straight out of Jesus's Sermon on the Mount in Matthew 5:14–16, was to declare not only that this Puritan settlement would strive to be a godly commonwealth and a beacon of light to the world but that it also would be judged by that same high standard, by the degree to which it faithfully carried out the terms of the "commission" that God had assigned it.

We might be tempted to read this as an expression of pride, as perhaps it was. But it was just as much an expression of humility, of a people choosing to subordinate their selfish desires to the accomplishment of their mission: to make a godly place in the New World, for the sake of the renewal of the Old.

So we can see in the contrast between Virginia and New England two of the contrasting aspects of the people and nation that were to come. In Virginia, the motives for settlement were largely material ones, while in Massachusetts Bay, they were frankly religious ones. This is not to say that there were no areas of overlap between the two. Virginia would have its distinguished churchmen and Massachusetts Bay its prosperous merchants. But it is fair to say that in the contrast between the two, we can see two very different principles – two different ways of understanding what is meant by "the good life" – on display.

Other British North American colonies were to come, too, and taken together, they formed a remarkably diverse group, covering a wide spectrum of possibilities. But most of them had in common an intentional quality. They were formed with some guiding purpose in mind.

Rhode Island was established under the leadership of Roger Williams, an intense Puritan minister who became a prophet of religious freedom, arguing that church and state should be kept completely separate, and that neither Massachusetts nor any other government had the right to overrule men's consciences in matters of faith.

Connecticut, by contrast, was a Puritan offshoot of both Plymouth and Massachusetts and contained the New Haven colony, which started out as the most strict Puritan settlement in all New England.

The colony of Pennsylvania was founded in 1682 to be a place for the Quakers, a radical religious group that arose out of England's political and religious conflicts. The Quakers, more formally known as the Society of Friends, went even further than the Puritans in rejecting the practices of the Catholic Church. They eliminated the clergy altogether, eliminated formal services, and eliminated reliance upon the text of the Bible. William Penn, its wealthy founder, considered his colony a "Holy Experiment" and offered complete freedom of worship to all. He promoted the colony tirelessly and encouraged the immigration of Germans and other non-English-speaking groups. His capital city was called "Philadelphia," a Greek name taken from the biblical book of Revelation, meaning the "City of Brotherly Love."

The last of the continental colonies, Georgia, established in 1732, was similarly inspired by brotherly love. It was the brainchild of a group of London humanitarians who were concerned over the problems of urban poverty, and particularly of those who were imprisoned for failure to pay off their debts. The humanitarians sought to obtain a grant of land from the king where these unfortunate debtors could be resettled to start their lives anew.

Not all the colonies reflected such large goals on the part of their founders. But a striking number of them did. In that respect, they recall many of the chief impulses behind the exploration and settlement of the Western world. They reflect the desire to renew the world, to restore it, to recover a unity that had been lost in the great unsettlement of Europe – or, equally, the desire to try out some of the religious and political ideals that had arisen out of that same unsettlement. All of these hopes and intentions found ample ground for their further exploration in the New World.

But let's be blunt. Each of these attempts failed in important respects to fulfill its original intentions. Every one of them. Puritan New England could not sustain itself; it had lost most of its religious zeal by the end of the seventeenth century. Quaker Philadelphia was no longer dominated by the Quakers by the time of the American Revolution, a victim of its own policies of toleration. Maryland was established to be a refuge for Catholics but quickly became dominated by Protestants. Georgia's experiment was a grand humanitarian plan that would renew the lives of desperate men, but it fell apart before the expiration of its royal charter, a victim of its own overly ambitious goals.

It is stories like these that made the historian Daniel Boorstin say that "the colonies were a disproving ground for utopias." He was right, but it would be a mistake to leave it at that. The impulse to hope, and to seek to realize one's hopes in the world, is the inmost spark of the human spirit, every bit as precious as life itself.

Much would be learned in the nearly two centuries of British North American colonial life, and much of what was learned came out of this same kind of back-and-forth between high hopes and hard realities. Colonial life was experimental, and even when experiments fail, something important can be learned from them.

Above all else, what was being learned in the English colonies was the habit of self-rule, developed in the lives of free colonists who were too distant from their colonial masters to be governable from afar. The example of the Mayflower Compact can serve as a model for all that was to come: free people coming together and, by their own initiative, establishing the institutions by which they would rule themselves. That habit of self-rule, grounded in English law and custom but reinforced by the many opportunities for experiment provided by a frontier society, was becoming a key element in their way of life.

4 · THINKING LIKE AMERICANS

IT SHOULD BE CLEAR by now that there was never a master plan for how the British colonies should be run. Instead, British colonial settlement was left mainly in the hands of private individuals and groups, pursuing their own goals. As it turned out, this very "plan-lessness" would be a major source of the English colonies' success, both economically and politically. That success illustrated an enduring truth. The results are likely to be far better when talented and energetic individuals are allowed to pursue their ambitions freely, without being dictated to by faraway rulers.

The English approach differed in this respect from that of the French and the Spanish. The difference was not entirely a matter of conscious English choice. It had a lot to do with the overall circumstances. England was distracted by its own internal political turmoil, especially during the extended struggles over the course of the seventeenth century between the English kings and Parliament for political supremacy. It wasn't possible to focus on governing overseas colonies when the most important matter at hand was something even more basic: determining what sort of government England would have at home and how much power the king should have.

Absolutism – the idea of concentrating political power in the hands of a single ruler – ran against the deepest traditions of the English, who had long insisted upon limiting the power of any king. These traditions went back at least to the restraints placed upon King John in the Magna Carta of 1215 and were expressed in the practices of the common law and the institution of Parliament. Not that absolutism had no backers in England, but efforts to impose absolutism there always faced stiff resistance. When James I ascended to the throne in 1603, and brought with him a belief in divine right, he thereby initiated several generations of heated and often violent conflict between the English kings and their Parliamentary opponents.

These struggles went on through much of the seventeenth century, seesawing back and forth through years of bitter and bloody civil strife – including the beheading of a king! – but finally culminating in the Glorious Revolution of 1688. That event overthrew James II, banished absolutism, established Parliamentary supremacy, produced a far-reaching Bill of Rights, and, along the way, provided an example for the American Revolution of 1776.

While all this commotion was going on, colonial affairs rested on the back burner of English policy. Efforts to control trade and make the colonies more profitable to England were ineffective. A series of Navigation Acts were passed by Parliament during those years, but none of them was ever enforced consistently or convincingly. Regulating trade was a big and complicated task, especially when it involved colonies an ocean away. The English simply did not have the means or the will to do the job. Hence Americans became accustomed to making their own decisions, receiving very loose direction from the mother country. Distance was the friend of self-rule.

Given the absence of a master plan, and the protective buffer of an ocean, experiments in American colonial self-government were free to flourish. To a remarkable degree, each of the colonies would undergo struggles very similar to the grand struggle being enacted in English politics. Colonial governors wrestled with their colonial assemblies, just as if they were little kings contending with little parliaments. Each colony was distinctive; but in many respects, each was an England in miniature. And more to the point, each had become entirely accustomed to governing itself.

Of course, the ability to participate in the political process in these colonies was very restricted when measured by our standards today. Women, Native Americans, and African Americans were rarely, if ever, permitted a role in political life. Neither were a great many white males. But it is important to keep that fact in correct perspective. The level of equality that we insist upon today did not yet exist anyplace in the world. In fact, a greater proportion of the American population could participate in elections and have a role in selecting their representatives than anywhere else on the planet. These colonists were acquiring the habit of self-rule, and they were not likely ever to want to give it up.

It would not be long before these different approaches to colonization would come into conflict. The rival European powers had largely been able to avoid getting into fights for most of the seventeenth century. There had been room enough for everyone. But that peaceful state of affairs could not last, as the great powers began to bump up against one another. In the seventy-five years after the Glorious Revolution, there would be four great European and intercolonial wars, the last of which, the Seven Years' War, would be particularly important to the future of America.

It came to be known in America as the French and Indian War and would last from 1754 to 1763. It would dramatically change the map of North America. It would also force a rethinking of the entire relationship between England and her colonies and an end to the "salutary neglect" policy. And that change, in turn, would pave the way to the American Revolution.

The French and Indian War began to take shape in North America in the early 1750s, when Pennsylvanian fur traders and land-hungry Virginians began to venture west into new territory, across the Allegheny Mountains and into the Ohio River Valley. This brought them into contact with French settlements and traders, and their presence produced an angry reaction. The French drove the British back and proceeded to construct forts in western Pennsylvania to protect their interests. The table was being set for more conflict.

A British delegation (including a twenty-one-year-old militia officer named George Washington) was sent to the French to settle the conflict, but it returned empty-handed. A subsequent mission to the area, led by Washington with the goal of building a fort at the site of present-day Pittsburgh, encountered armed French resistance and suffered a humiliating defeat in the Battle of Fort Necessity. Then, in 1755, British general Edward Braddock, dispatched to Virginia to take care of the situation, after hacking his way through the wilderness of the upper Potomac, found himself soundly defeated by guerrilla forces made up of a combination of Ojibwa Indians and French soldiers. Braddock's forces sustained some nine hundred casualties, including the loss of his own life.

Such disappointing results caused British prime minister William Pitt to turn up the power and make America the principal field of conflict with France in the Seven Years' War. Pitt recognized far better than most of his contemporaries the enormous ultimate value of North America, and accordingly, he poured resources from the national treasury into the cause – lavishly, even recklessly, in ways that would weigh on his country's future. He mobilized forty-five thousand troops for the purpose and invested a lot of money – the economist Adam Smith estimated it at £90 million, which would be many billions of dollars today – all the while treating the colonists as partners in the war enterprise. His efforts bore fruit in 1759 with a series of military victories, at Fort Niagara, Lake Champlain, and, most decisively of all, on September 13, 1759, at Quebec City. It was there that General James Wolfe made short work of the French infantry on a plateau known as the Plains of Abraham, an hour-long battle that effectively put an end to French ambitions for North America.

The war was formally concluded with the Treaty of Paris in February 1763, making French North America a thing of the past, except for two tiny islands off the coast of Newfoundland. England, now more properly known as Great Britain, took over Canada and the eastern half of the Mississippi valley. It was a great victory and seemed to cement British dominance in the New World.

Every great victory in war means the creation of a new set of problems in peace. The French and Indian War was no exception

An eighteenth-century map showing British possessions in North America following the French and Indian War.

to the rule. This victory would mean the end of the era of "benign neglect," the British policy of leaving the colonies alone, a policy that was the source of so much creativity and freedom for the colonies. After this war, as we'll soon see, such loose American independence could no longer be allowed to continue. The British Parliament would not stand for it.

The Americans had an opposite response, for the war had produced a surge of pride among American colonials. They had shared the experience of fighting a war together. That had generated in many of them the first stirrings of American *national* sentiment, the feeling that there might be something binding all the colonies together, something more than just their shared British origins, language, and cultural heritage.

But it was the British who had won the war, not the Americans, and it was the British who had paid for it – at mammoth expense, which burdened the nation with millions of pounds in additional debt, the equivalent today of many billions of dollars. In fact, the war doubled Britain's national debt. As a result, it seemed inevitable that things would have to change. As Adam Smith observed, it was no longer possible for the colonies to be considered "provinces of the British empire" that "contribute neither revenue nor military force toward the support of the empire." In other words, the days of the colonies getting a free ride – receiving British military protection without being required to pay taxes as British citizens – were over.

It made sense to devise a system within which the Americans would pay their fair share. But the problem was *how* to do it. How to go about the business of knitting together the British Empire more tightly, while maintaining the profoundly English tradition of allowing a maximum degree of self-rule in its parts? This was not going to be an easy problem to solve.

War was not the only common experience beginning to draw the colonies together. Religion was another. It's true that by the beginning of the eighteenth century, the religious zeal that had motivated the first Puritan and Quaker settlers began to fade, as the colonies became more settled and comfortable, less convinced of their dependency on God. But that period of religious indifference did not last.

Beginning in the 1730s, waves of religious and spiritual revival began to sweep up and down the colonies along the North American coast, a mass movement called the Great Awakening. This was a movement of renewal that would transform the church life of the colonies and introduce a more earnest and heartfelt approach to worship.

The fuse for this explosion of religious energy was lit by a brilliant American-born theologian named Jonathan Edwards, whose vivid preaching at the Congregational church in Northampton, Massachusetts, in the earlier years of the 1730s became famous and, according to many accounts, had transformed the frontier of

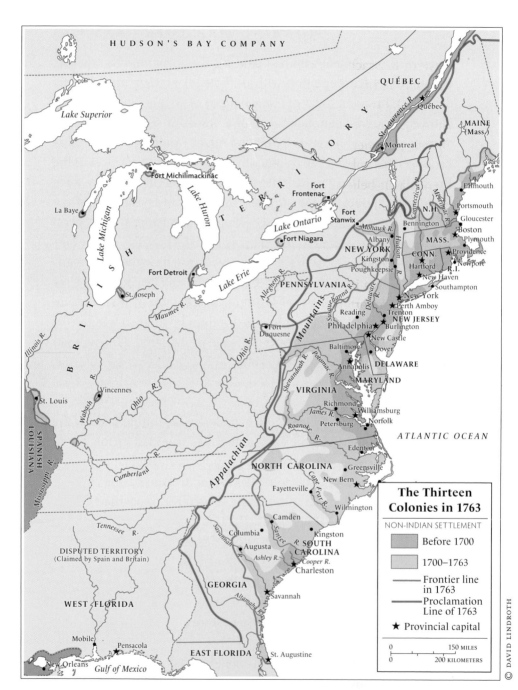

A schematic of the territorial results of the French and Indian War, including the proclamation line of 1763. The map overlies boundaries of present-day states.

western Massachusetts from a spiritual desert to a land of intense religious activity.

But the most influential preacher of the day was the itinerant minister George Whitefield. A highly dramatic and golden-voiced British preacher, he arrived in Philadelphia in 1739 and traveled through the colonies, everywhere drawing enormous crowds of enthusiastic believers who were seeking the "new birth" of sudden religious conversion. Whitefield's phenomenal voice was so powerful that he could hold the rapt attention of crowds as large as twenty thousand. His success was a measure not only of his amazing talents but of how hungry the colonists were for his spiritual message.

Aside from its influence on religious life, the Great Awakening had other important side effects. It was a shared event that had been felt throughout the colonies and was experienced as something fresh and new – a form of religious expression different from the practices that the colonists' forebears had brought with them. It emphasized individual conversion and behavior more than correct doctrines and forms. It was democratic, with an appeal directly to the common people – to laborers, servants, farmers, and mechanics. It was often more emotional than intellectual and had little regard for tradition. It often led to divisions within churches, between those who favored the old ways and those who insisted upon the new. It made the choices of individuals, operating independently of church leaders, one of the defining features of American religion.

But religion was not the only current running in the world of ideas. This was also the age of the Enlightenment, the influential European movement devoted to reason and science. You might think that the ideas of the Enlightenment stood apart from religion entirely. After all, the Enlightenment understood the world as a rational and orderly place governed by natural laws that could be discovered and made known to the human mind through the careful methods of modern experimental science. America would prove to be an especially good place for the Enlightenment to take root, since America was a new land, a land of new societies, a land of nature rather than one of rooted traditions. It was no coincidence that America would become the first place on earth where the idea that each individual person possesses natural rights – rights that derived from nature or God, and not from the hand of any king or agency of government – would take hold strongly.

It is also the case that, despite their differences, these two currents – the Great Awakening and the Enlightment – had important features in common. Both were very American. They shared a suspicion of traditional institutions. They showed little reverence for established authority, whether in the church or in politics. Both understood themselves as an expression of the spirit of liberty. No less than the Enlightenment, the Great Awakening weakened the power of all traditional churches and clergy, Protestant and Catholic alike, and indeed of all figures of authority, while making religious life dependent on the judgments of each person's free conscience.

Such changes would have effects far beyond matters of religion. Among other things, they would make it easier for the American colonists, who were beginning to think of themselves as a distinct people, to contemplate becoming something new, through an act of rebellion against their king and empire. The stage was being set for just such an act.

5 · A REVOLUTION OF SELF-RULE

BEFORE THE AMERICAN REVOLUTION, the British colonists thought of themselves as British subjects of the British Crown. How did they reach the point where they were ready to declare, and fight for, their independence? Let's try to explain it.

After the French and Indian War, a huge new British Empire was encircling the globe. This meant that the problem of how to organize the empire, which had been delayed so many times, couldn't be put off any longer, particularly with respect to the American colonies. Theoretically, those colonies were entirely subject to king and Parliament. But in practice, that authority had never been effectively exercised.

In fact, Parliament had never tried to raise revenue in America, and prominent colonial figures like Benjamin Franklin firmly opposed the idea, stating that doing so without the colonists' consent would be like "raising contributions in an enemy's country," rather than "taxing Englishmen for their own benefit." And that was precisely how the colonists saw the matter. But that did not mean that Parliament had no right to raise such taxes, should it ever choose to do so. Under the policy of "salutary neglect," the matter had been left dangling. That would not continue to be the case for much longer.

Even before the conclusion of the war in 1763, the British were moving toward tightening up on the colonies. One notable example occurred in 1761, when the use of general search warrants (also known as writs of assistance) was authorized as a way of allowing British officials to crack down on colonial smugglers who were trading with the French in the West Indies. This meant that agents now could enter any place for any reason, even a person's home, in search of evidence of illegal trade.

Americans reacted in horror to this invasion of their privacy and smashing of their rights. A group of merchants hired Boston lawyer James Otis to challenge the writs in court, and Otis proceeded to give an eloquent, carefully researched, and powerfully argued oration before the Massachusetts Superior Court. It was one of the great speeches of early American history; and although Otis spoke for nearly five hours, he was, said John Adams, like "a flame of fire," and his speech echoed in the minds of all who heard it. Unfortunately, he lost the case, but his argument that the very institution of the writs violated the British constitution was an argument that supplied an important precedent for the years ahead.

Another burdensome issue facing the British was what to do about the lands west of the Appalachian Mountains that were still inhabited by Indian tribes. The victory over the French had given British colonial settlers a new reason to expand into Indian lands; but such invasions led to a bloody reaction, known as Pontiac's Rebellion, in which the tribes attempted to push white settlers back across the mountains. The rebellion failed, but the British wanted to prevent any repeat experience. They adopted a new western policy: by the terms of the Royal Proclamation of 1763, no settlers were to cross an imaginary line running across the tops of the Appalachian Mountains.

This edict was unpopular with American colonists, but the public response to it was relatively mild. That was partly because it did not directly involve taxation and partly because settlers felt free to defy it. It appeared to be yet another grand but ineffective British measure, like those that had been tried and failed in the past. But there would be a far more intense reaction against the measures soon put forward under the leadership of Prime Minister George Grenville, a stubborn, hardheaded accountant who was determined to make the prosperous Americans pay some of the cost for their own protection.

The Sugar Act, proposed in 1764, placed tariffs (taxes) on sugar, tea, coffee, and wines, all of which were products that Americans needed to import. Those accused of violating the act would be tried before British naval officers in a court based in Canada, in which they would not have the right to be presumed innocent, as was the case in most American courts. And in a further intrusion into the colonies' customary practices of self-governance, the Currency Act of 1764 sought to end the colonies' practice of printing their own paper money.

Both of these measures failed to raise money for Britain. But the message was clear: after the French and Indian War, and under the leadership of Grenville, the era of Britain's easygoing inattention to the colonies was coming to an end. And there was much more to come.

The pace of intrusion quickened even more in 1765 when Parliament produced the Stamp Act, which required that stamps be purchased and attached to legal documents and printed matter of all kinds, ranging from newspapers to playing cards. The same year, Grenville directed Parliament to pass the Quartering Act, which required the colonial legislatures to supply British troops with barracks and food wherever they were – in effect, another form of taxation. The justification offered for both measures was that they were ways that the colonists could help pay for their own self-defense. But the Stamp Act did not work either; in fact, it did not produce any revenue at all. The colonists simply refused to obey it.

Why did they react so strongly? For one thing, they resisted because this act meant that they had to pay taxes directly and raised in their minds the possibility that the larger concept of self-rule might be threatened. Protests against the Stamp Act were everywhere. There was a flood of pamphlets, speeches, resolutions, and public meetings, at which the cry of "no taxation without representation" was heard far and wide. Some protests turned violent, with British stamp officials being harassed, vandalized, and hanged in effigy and the stamps themselves confiscated and burned. By the time the law was to take effect in November 1765, it was already a dead letter.

Once again, Grenville and Parliament had misjudged the situation. Grenville invented a doctrine called "virtual representation" to explain how it was that the colonists could be represented in Parliament even if they could not send their own popularly elected members to take part in it. In this view, the members of Parliament had the right to speak for the interests of all British subjects, rather than for the interests only of the district that elected them. Some Britons found this idea persuasive, but the colonists, deeply rooted as they were in the habit of self-rule, dismissed it as rubbish, incompatible with the principle that government derives its just powers from the consent of the governed.

More and more of them became convinced that Grenville's aggressive actions would overturn their accustomed way of life and impose the same tyranny that the English themselves had fought against so valiantly in the seventeenth century, and from which Parliament had finally saved them in the Glorious Revolution. It was as if the same history was being reenacted, with many of the same danger signs in evidence.

Troubling questions arose in their minds. Why were the British imposing a standing army in the western lands, if not to confine and suppress the colonists? Why were the new courts overriding the traditional English commitment to trial by jury, if not for the purpose of replacing local liberty with the heavy hand of the Empire? Why was Parliament infringing upon the colonial assemblies' "power of the purse" (the power to tax and spend public money), thereby taking away from them one of the most basic of English rights? The colonists had a pattern close at hand in their own history that could make sense of these things.

Finally, the British appeared to pull back from the brink. In 1766, Grenville was dismissed from office and replaced by the more flexible and sympathetic Marquis of Rockingham. In addition, Parliament repealed the Stamp Act, a move for which Americans were grateful, and which immediately eased tensions. But what Parliament was giving with one hand it was taking away with the other. On the same day that it repealed the Stamp Act, it passed a Declaratory Act stating that Parliament's power over the colonies was unlimited in principle and that it *could* enact whatever law it wished "to bind the colonies and people of America." This was more than just a face-saving gesture. It was stating, under the cover of what appeared to be a retreat, a very strong assertion of sovereignty, a principle to which Parliament could turn in future battles.

For the British had not abandoned the goal of reordering the empire, and that inevitably meant finding a way to tax the colonies. The next nine years of conflict represented a steadily intensifying effort on their part to establish the imperial control that had so far eluded them, met by a steadily mounting resistance on the colonists' part, and accompanied by a growing awareness on the colonial side that the issues separating them from the mother country were becoming deeper by the day.

The Declaratory Act offered clear evidence that, beneath all the particular points of conflict between England and America, there were two sets of very different ideas: different ideas about the proper place of America in the emerging imperial system and about the meaning of words like *self-rule, representation, constitution,* and *sovereignty.* It was a genuine debate, in which both sides had legitimate arguments. But it did not help that, as time went by, British leaders seemed less inclined to listen to the colonial perspective and more inclined to crush it.

Following in the years after the Stamp Act controversy was a series of inconclusive conflicts that only seemed to heighten the inevitability of armed conflict. The next round began in 1767, when British official Charles Townshend introduced a new revenue plan, which included taxes on glass, paint, lead, paper, and tea imported into the colonies. To this, the colonists responded with boycotts of British goods, with efforts to encourage colonial manufacturing, and with a growing radical resistance movement headed by firebrand agitators like the brewer Samuel Adams of Boston.

Eventually, after the 1770 Boston Massacre resulted in the deaths of five Americans at the hands of British soldiers, Parliament repealed all the Townshend duties, except the one on tea. Things settled down somewhat until 1773, when a group of sixteen disguised colonists dumped a load of East India Company tea into Boston Harbor, thus carrying out the famous Boston Tea Party. This immediately caused an enraged response from Parliament, in the form of four Coercive Acts, or, as the colonists called them, Intolerable Acts. These were designed to take control of Massachusetts's legal and economic system, turn Boston into an occupied city, and thereby single it out for humiliation, making it an example to all the others.

This divide-and-conquer strategy did not work either. Instead, it caused the other colonies to rise up and rally to Boston's cause. They began by sharing supplies and increasing boycotts of British goods. Soon they were organizing a first-ever Continental Congress, which would represent the interests of all the colonies – a clear step in the direction of a political union.

When the Continental Congress met in Philadelphia in September 1774, it endorsed the various forms of lawful resistance to the Coercive Acts, particularly the boycotts, and endorsed a Declaration of American Rights, which expressed the colonists' shared belief in the limited authority of Parliament. Exactly how to define the extent of that limitation, however, was a matter about which there would be disagreement. Did Parliament retain the right to regulate trade alone – or was even that right now endangered, as the Boston lawyer John Adams, a cousin of Sam Adams, asserted?

In the meantime, the boycott movement was becoming more effective, tapping into the patriotic passions of thousands of ordinary Americans who were willing to express their alarm at the British threats to American liberty. It was the same common people – farmers and working men – who volunteered to serve in militias, such as the Minute Men of Massachusetts, and for the same reasons.

This was no longer the behavior of loyal subjects but increasingly that of liberty-loving citizens yearning to breathe free and restore self-rule.

A profound shift was taking place. As John Adams said, reflecting many years later on the events he had lived through, "The Revolution was effected before the war commenced. The Revolution was in the minds and hearts of the people; a change in their religious sentiments of their duties and obligations." The people of America had been inclined to have reverence for their king and their British institutions. But when they saw their British leaders behaving like tyrants, their affections changed dramatically. "This radical change in the principles, opinions, sentiments, and affections of the people," declared Adams, "was the real American Revolution."

The direction of this gathering storm was clear to the British leadership, which was more willing than ever to have a showdown with the colonies. Britain's King George III put it bluntly: "The New England governments are in a state of rebellion. Blows must decide whether they are to be subject to this country or independent." In this respect, he faithfully reflected the general state of British opinion, which wanted to bring to a swift end what looked increasingly like sheer rebellion.

The fuse of war was lit at last in April 1775, when orders reached the royal governor of Massachusetts, Thomas Gage, to move aggressively to stop the rebellion. Gage decided to march seven hundred red-coated British troops to Concord, a town about twenty miles west of Boston, where he would seize a militia supply depot that had been established by the Patriot forces. Along the way, in the town of Lexington, the British encountered a ragtag group of seventy Minute Men. It was dawn, but the men were there because they had been warned, by the famous midnight ride of Paul Revere, that the British were coming.

After some taunting shouts and argument, the Patriot militiamen were beginning to withdraw – and then a shot was fired, leading the British to fire on the group, killing eight of them. Then the British went on to Concord, where they encountered half-empty store-houses and stiff resistance, as alerted militiamen swarmed into the area. After losing fourteen men in a skirmish at Concord's North Bridge, the British began to retreat to Boston and faced deadly fire along the entire bloody way back. In the end, the British lost three times as many men as the Americans.

So the war had begun; the conflict spread to Fort Ticonderoga in upper New York and to the hills overlooking Boston, where the Americans again showed their military mettle, inflicting more than a thousand casualties on a startled British army in the Battle of Bunker Hill. But the war's objectives were not yet clear, since independence had not yet been declared.

Even some who identified wholeheartedly with the Patriot cause still found it impossible to contemplate such a final break. John Dickinson of Pennsylvania had expressed their worries at the time of the Townshend Acts this way: "If once we are separated from our mother country, what new form of government shall we accept, or when shall we find another Britain to supply our loss?" It seemed to him that the American colonies were too weak and divided to make themselves into a nation and that the ties of common culture with Britain were too many and too strong to be broken without a terrible loss. "Torn from the body to which we are united, by religion, liberty, laws, affections, relations, language, and commerce, we must," he feared, "bleed at every vein."

And that was not all. There might be even worse fates in store than being tyrannized by the British Crown. There might be domination by other hostile powers. And the disturbances in Boston and elsewhere suggested the possibility of mob rule and of a breakdown of law and order altogether. It was a frightening and uncertain time.

Several more things had to happen for the movement to independence to become unstoppable. First, the British government refused to consider any form of compromise. King George III angrily rejected a peacemaking appeal known as the Olive Branch Petition, written by Dickinson, refusing even to look at it and choosing instead to label the colonists "open and avowed enemies." Then the king began to recruit mercenary (hired) soldiers from Germany to fight the Americans, a gesture that the colonists regarded as both insulting and heartless, a way of signaling that they were no longer fellow Englishmen.

Finally, there was the publication of Thomas Paine's pamphlet *Common Sense*. It argued openly for independence, directing the colonists' anger not at the Parliament but at the very personal figure of the king himself. Paine attacked not only the current monarch (whom he mocked as a "Royal Brute" and a "Pharaoh") but the very idea of monarchy itself. Paine himself was a British man who had only been in America a year, a rootless and luckless soul in his late thirties who had failed at nearly everything else he had attempted. But when it came to political agitation and stirring language, he was very much a success.

He had brought with him a deep commitment to the ideal of self-rule and a vivid prose style that made the case for independence with greater power and grace than anyone before him. His pamphlet became known to most everyone in the colonies and sold more than 150,000 copies within the first three months of 1776. Its effect was electrifying. "*Common Sense* is working a powerful change in the minds of men," admitted George Washington, who would soon be a leader of the Patriot cause. Paine had connected the dots as no one before him had done and had brought sharp definition to an unsettled situation. He made the path forward unmistakably clear.

Finally, at the urging of the colonial governments, the Continental Congress began to move decisively toward independence. Richard Henry Lee introduced a motion on June 7 "that these United Colonies are, and of right ought to be, free and independent states." The resolution passed on July 2, which really should be the day that Americans celebrate Independence Day. But it was two days later, on the Fourth of July, that the Congress adopted the

Declaration of Independence, a remarkable document written mainly by the thirty-three-year-old Thomas Jefferson of Virginia.

The Declaration served several functions. On one level, it was a press release to the world, listing the specific reasons for the Americans' actions. But it also was a presentation of the key elements of the American political philosophy. It was, and has continued to be, a document of many dimensions, with importance not only to America in the eighteenth century but to the people of the entire world.

Reflecting on the matter nearly fifty years later, Jefferson explicitly denied that there was any originality in his ideas. Instead, he sought to express the things about which nearly all Americans agreed. The Declaration said it was a "self-evident" truth that all men were created equal and were endowed by their Creator – and not by their government or any other human authority – with certain rights, including "life, liberty, and the pursuit of happiness."

Governments existed to protect these rights and derived their powers from the consent of the governed – a crisp statement of the basic principle of self-rule. When a government failed to protect those rights and failed to reflect the consent of the governed, when it revealed a "design" to deprive the colonists of their liberty, it was no longer a just regime, and the people had the right to abolish and replace it – which is to say, they had a right of revolution.

A long list of grievances followed, laying nearly all the blame at the feet of the king, just as Thomas Paine had done in *Common Sense*. "He has refused his Assent to Laws.... He has dissolved representative houses.... He has obstructed the Administration of Justice.... He has kept among us standing armies.... He has plundered our seas, ravaged our Coasts, burnt our towns, and destroyed the lives of our people.... A Prince whose character is thus marked by every act which may define a tyrant is unfit to be the ruler of a free people."

The grievances built forcefully to the Declaration's inescapable conclusion, echoing the words of Lee's motion: "That these United Colonies are, and of Right ought to be free and independent states; that they are absolved from all Allegiance to the British Crown, and … have full power to levy War, conclude Peace, contract Alliances, establish Commerce, and to do all other Acts and Things which Independent States may of right do."

The Declaration was a magnificent and enduringly influential document. It has been read and admired around the world, and is admired to this day, as one of the greatest of all charters of human dignity and freedom. Its eloquence gave immense help to the American colonial cause, while at the same time strengthening the cause of liberty in France and other places around the world.

Yet it left many questions unanswered. The document was very clear about the form of union it was rejecting. But what kind of union was it embracing? What would it mean to have a postcolonial union of free and independent states? Wasn't that a contradiction? How was it possible to be both united and independent?

And then there were those stirring words "all men are created equal." What did they actually mean? Did they mean "equality" in only the narrowest sense – that the American colonists were in no way *politically* inferior to the arrogant British, who were trying to deprive them of their rights? Or was there a larger sense to those words? Did it include everyone? Did it apply only to males, or did the term *men* include women? Was this equality compatible with the obvious facts of inequality – the existence of differences in strength, size, wealth, talent, beauty, and so on – that one can see every day in the life of every human society?

And what about the growing stain of slavery, the very existence of which called into question the sincerity of the words Jefferson had written? Jefferson himself owned slaves, despite his moral misgivings about the institution of slavery. What did *he* think he was saying when he wrote those words? How could those words allow for an institution that permitted ownership in human flesh? How to answer the taunts of men like those who sneered that the Americans were "hypocritical friends of liberty who buy and sell and whip their fellow men as if they were brutes," but then turn around "and absurdly complain that they are enslaved"?

But all these questions lay in the future, and answering them would be one of the principal tasks facing the new nation for the next 250 years. The Revolution was fought by imperfect individuals who had a mixture of motives, including the purely economic motives of some who just didn't want to pay taxes.

Yet self-rule was at the heart of it all. Self-rule had been the basis for the flourishing of these colonies. Self-rule was the basis for their revolution. Self-rule would continue to be a central element in the American experiment in all the years to come.

Perhaps nothing better illustrates the central importance of self-rule than an interview given in 1843 by Captain Levi Preston, a soldier who fought the British at Concord in 1775 and was interviewed at the age of ninety-one by a young Mellen Chamberlain:

"Captain Preston, why did you go to the Concord Fight, the 19th of April, 1775?"

The old man, bowed beneath the weight of years, raised himself upright, and turning to me said: "Why did I go?"

"Yes," I replied; "my histories tell me that you men of the Revolution took up arms against 'intolerable oppressions.'"

"What were they? Oppressions? I didn't feel them."

"What, were you not oppressed by the Stamp Act?"

"I never saw one of those stamps, and always understood that Governor Bernard put them all in Castle William. I am certain I never paid a penny for one of them."

"Well, what then about the tea-tax?"

"Tea-tax! I never drank a drop of the stuff; the boys threw it all overboard."

"Then I suppose you had been reading Harrington or Sidney and Locke about the eternal principles of liberty."

"Never heard of 'em. We read only the Bible, the Catechism, Watts's Psalms and Hymns, and the Almanack."

"Well, then, what was the matter? and what did you mean in going to the fight?"

"Young man, what we meant in going for those red-coats was this: we always had governed ourselves, and we always meant to. They didn't mean we should."

And that, concluded Chamberlain, was the ultimate philosophy of the American Revolution. It was a revolution of self-rule.

6 · A WORLD TURNED UPSIDE DOWN

DECLARING INDEPENDENCE was the easy part. It was not hard to celebrate the cause of independence in ringing words. It was not hard to manage a few small and scattered military triumphs, even if they depended on the element of surprise and were little more than pinpricks to annoy the British and frustrate their intentions. But it did not take long before the enormous size of the task ahead became clear and the earlier warnings of men like John Dickinson – a Patriot who had nevertheless opposed the Declaration, calling it a "skiff made of paper" – began to sound prophetic. How on earth did the American revolutionary leaders imagine that they could prevail against the greatest military power in the world?

They went into the struggle with huge disadvantages. To begin with, the country, which was hardly even a country yet, was not fully united in embracing the revolutionary cause. We often assume that everyone in the colonies was solidly on board for independence, but that was very far from being the case. It is hard to know for sure about the numbers, but perhaps as many as one-third of Americans remained loyal to the Crown and opposed the Revolution; another third seemed to be indifferent as to the outcome. Even the remaining third, which supported independence, had varied reasons for doing so. And the emerging country did not yet have an effective form of national political organization. As we've already seen, the Declaration itself was unclear as to exactly what kind of union these "free and independent states" were going to form together.

In addition, there could be no guarantee that the unity declared in summer 1776 would survive in a hard and punishing war. The Americans could field only the most basic, ill-trained, and poorly supplied army. They had no navy to speak of. They had little money and no obvious way of raising funds to build and support these essential military components. The deck seemed to be stacked against them.

The very day on which the Continental Congress voted on independence, the British were easily able to land, without facing any resistance, a large number of troops on Staten Island at the entrance to New York Harbor, the first installment in what would by August be a force of more than thirty thousand. American victory under such circumstances was beginning to look like a pipe dream.

But the Americans had certain very real advantages, and those would soon become clear. First, they were playing defense. They would not need to take the war across the ocean to the motherland of Britain to win; they needed only to hold on long enough at home to wear out the enemy's willingness to fight. With time on their side, the Americans could lose most of the battles but still win the war. In addition, other European powers would be happy to see an increasingly dominant Britain be dealt a severe blow. It was entirely possible that the colonies would find allies among Britain's enemies. If France, Britain's perpetual foe, could be persuaded to support the American cause directly – well, that could make all the difference and compensate for the weaknesses of the American position. So the situation was far from hopeless.

The Americans also had a second advantage. They were blessed with a great leader in the person of George Washington, a man of extraordinarily fine character who enjoyed the admiration of nearly all Americans. He was a proven Patriot who had strongly opposed the recent actions of the British Parliament and was committed to preserving the colonists' rights and freedoms. He was willing to leave a pleasant life at his Mount Vernon estate to lead the colonial opposition. When he showed up at the Second Continental Congress in Philadelphia, he was wearing his military uniform, signaling that he was ready to fight for the colonial cause. The Congress acted accordingly, making him commander in chief of the Continental Army in June 1775. He accepted the position on condition that he receive no pay for it.

His insistence upon that condition tells us a great deal about the man. Courageous, wise, tireless, and incorruptible, George Washington was the best man to lead the war effort. He had extensive military experience and looked the part of a natural leader, impressively tall and muscular, with a dignified gravity in his bearing that led all to treat him with instinctive respect. But even more, he was known and admired as a man who self-consciously modeled himself on the classical republican ideal of the unselfish, virtuous, and public-spirited leader – the kind of man who disdained material rewards and sought the public good instead. Like a great many other Americans of his day, Washington was deeply influenced by Joseph Addison's 1712 play *Cato, a Tragedy*, a popular drama depicting the virtuous life of its subject, the ancient Roman senator Cato the Younger, who devoted his life to opposing the tyranny of Julius Caesar. Washington saw the play performed a great many times and frequently quoted it in his correspondence. Cato's example was one he always sought to follow.

The greatest immediate challenge facing Washington was that of creating a disciplined and effective American army. This was no easy task, and it would continue to be a problem through the entire conflict. The numbers of troops at his disposal were constantly changing. In August 1776, he had twenty-eight thousand men under his command; by December, that number had shrunk to a mere three thousand.

What had happened? Washington's troops had been driven from New York City by British forces under the command of Major General William Howe and were forced to flee into New Jersey and, eventually, Pennsylvania. Along the way, a great many militiamen simply deserted and went home. It was not the only time this would happen. The army's morale and numbers were always unstable, prone to peaks of hope and valleys of despair, depending on how the war seemed to be going at any given time. Washington had to keep a cool head through these constant fluctuations and frustrations.

The winter of 1776–77 that lay ahead would be an extremely harsh one, a gloomy valley of discouragement. But the Patriots' morale would be lifted by the appearance of another work from the pen of Thomas Paine, the first in a series of pamphlets called *The American Crisis*, tailor-made for the discontents of that moment. It began with his famous inspirational words: "These are the times that try men's souls: The summer soldier and the sunshine patriot will, in this crisis, shrink from the service of his country; but he that stands by it now deserves the love and thanks of man and woman."

Yes, the immediate future looked grim. But that was even more reason to hunker down and push ahead. "The harder the conflict," Paine insisted, "the more glorious the triumph." Once again, his words worked their magic. Washington ordered that they be read aloud to the army encampments, and they had the desired effect, rousing the fighting spirit of his men. For a second time in one year, Paine had made a great gift to the colonial cause.

And then, on Christmas night 1776, Washington struck back at the British. He led a force across the Delaware River and surprised at dawn a sleeping force of Hessians at Trenton, New Jersey; then, a week later, his forces enjoyed a similar triumph, repulsing a British force at Princeton – two small victories, but perhaps a sign of good things to come. They made it possible for the American soldiers to go into the winter months, which they spent at Morristown in the hills of New Jersey, with a feeling of momentum.

It appeared that the Americans would not be defeated quickly, a fact that not only greatly encouraged the Patriots and aided their recruiting but discouraged the British and those loyal to them. Despite a brutal, smallpox-ridden winter at Morristown, during which the army shrank to a mere thousand men, the coming of spring brought a flow of fresh recruits. Washington could resume the fight against Howe.

As it turned out, the coming year of 1777 would be crucial in determining the outcome of the war. The British had formulated a complex plan that would have the effect of cutting New England off from the rest of the colonies, through three coordinated assaults on American positions. Had the elements of the plan succeeded, they might have ended the colonial insurrection then and there. But all three assaults failed miserably.

The most important of them involved the colorful British general John "Gentleman Johnny" Burgoyne, commanding the northern forces, who was to move his men down from Canada and across Lake Champlain toward Albany. He successfully crossed the lake and occupied the abandoned Fort Ticonderoga on the lake's southern end. But when he tried to go farther, the effort, which was slowed by an immense baggage train that included thirty carts carrying Burgoyne's lavish wardrobe and supplies of champagne, became bogged down in the dense woods north of Saratoga. The American forces swelled in numbers and enthusiasm as volunteers and militia flocked to the area, and eventually Burgoyne found himself hopelessly surrounded and forced to surrender on October 17. Some fifty-seven hundred British troops were taken prisoner. It was a very big triumph for the Americans.

In fact, it was a victory of great importance, a key turning point. After Saratoga, the war's eventual outcome would not be much in doubt, even though there was much fighting yet to be done. That was because the victory at Saratoga was the signal the French had been waiting for. It was a clear indication that the Americans were up to the fight and that it might therefore be in the interest of the French to involve themselves on the side of the Americans and help them administer a bitter setback to their old enemies, the British. After having lost their North American empire to the British just a few years before, the French wanted to return the favor. It would be a sweet revenge to deprive the British of their North American colonies and thereby greatly diminish their power in the world.

Fearing this very prospect, Lord North made a desperate offer to the colonies. He would repeal all the offensive acts passed in the years before 1775 and promise never to tax the colonies. But it was too little too late, and the offer was flatly rejected. Instead, as a direct consequence of the American victory at Saratoga, the French extended diplomatic recognition to the United States and concluded a treaty of alliance.

The French had already been aiding the colonial cause with gunpowder and other supplies. In 1778, they would join the war effort on the American side, as would the Spanish and the Dutch. This would mean not only additional trained troops but the assistance of the French navy, which could make it possible to challenge British naval superiority. The United States would soon have the powerful new friends it had been hoping for.

But that lay in the future, just over the horizon. In the meantime, the horrendous winter of 1777–78 represented a low point for Washington's army. It was encamped at Valley Forge, eighteen miles outside Philadelphia, where its men would be overwhelmed by exposure, hunger, and disease. The army's very existence hung by a thread. The Marquis de Lafayette, a French aristocrat who had volunteered to fight with the Americans, observed that "the unfortunate soldiers ... had neither coats, nor hats, nor shirts, nor shoes; their feet and legs froze till they grew black, and it was often necessary to amputate them." More than twenty-five hundred soldiers died by the end of February 1778, and another thousand deserted. Another seven thousand were too ill for duty. Faith in Washington's leadership ability was put to a severe test.

But after the arrival of General Friedrich Wilhelm von Steuben on February 23 to begin training the army, things began to turn around. The army miraculously regained its fighting spirit. Von Steuben was a pro; he had been a member of the Prussian army, had served on the General Staff of Frederick the Great, and believed in the American cause. He immediately began to put the American troops through an intense regimen of drilling. By May, he had made them into a military force. Encouraged by news of the French military alliance, and by a promise of extra pay from the Congress, the Continental army was ready to move ahead.

In summer 1778, Washington's forces were strong enough to go after the withdrawing British forces in New Jersey. After an inconclusive engagement at Monmouth Court House, the middle region of the colonies settled into stalemate – and stalemate was nearly as good as victory, under the circumstances. In the meantime, there was good news on the western frontier. The daring young Virginia militiaman George Rogers Clark led 175 frontiersmen down the Ohio River in flatboats and, on July 4, surprised the British-held Kaskaskia and captured it without firing a shot. Clark in short order took the garrison at Cahokia and then occupied Vincennes in present-day Indiana. Washington enthusiastically hailed these victories, which offered further proof to the French of the fighting effectiveness of their new American allies.

But not everything went so well. In late 1780, the British turned their attention to the southern colonies (which were important to them as sources of staple crops and raw materials) and captured Savannah and Charleston. The latter debacle was the worst American defeat of the war. Then, seeking to cut the Carolinas off from external sources of aid, British general Charles Cornwallis took his force of seventy-two hundred men northward, heading toward Virginia and ending up in Yorktown, a small port city strategically located near the mouth of the Chesapeake Bay. They would be safe there, he believed, since the Americans lacked a serious navy to challenge them by water and lacked sufficient troops in the area to threaten them by land.

Both assumptions proved dead wrong. Cornwallis soon found himself trapped in the pincers of a combined operation, coming at him from both sea and land. First, French Admiral Comte de Grasse's fleet came up from its Caribbean base to decisively defeat the British navy in September 1781 in the Battle of the Chesapeake. De Grasse was then able to blockade the coast, while in the meantime ferrying in troops to join those already in place outside the town. In time, the American and French troops gathered outside Yorktown numbered more than sixteen thousand, more than twice the size of

Cornwallis's army. He was trapped, was hopelessly outmaneuvered, and had no choice but to surrender.

On October 19, he did so. It is said that, as his forces marched out, the British band struck up a familiar English ballad, "The World Turned Upside Down."

So it must have seemed to Cornwallis and his men. With their surrender, the war was effectively over, and the impossible had happened: America had won. The world *had* been turned upside down. Peace talks would begin soon thereafter, concluding with the Treaty of Paris signed on September 3, 1783. This treaty confirmed that the American independence that had been declared in 1776, and that had been so persistently and courageously sought, had been won – despite long odds, over seven long and hard years of struggle.

Now the greatest struggle of all, the challenge of making American independence work, would begin.

7 · THE CRITICAL PERIOD

FIRST, A CONFESSION. We actually don't know for certain whether the band at Yorktown played "The World Turned Upside Down"; there is no historical record of the matter. It might just be a well-established legend. But if it was, it was a very meaningful one. The words of the song not only served to taunt the defeated British. They also raised unsettling questions for the Americans about where the revolutionary journey was taking them. If this was to be a revolution, how complete a revolution was it to be? Was, in fact, the world being turned upside down – or merely right side up?

The second possibility might have seemed more likely. As we've seen, the most influential arguments for revolution did not speak of radical change as the chief aim. Instead, they spoke of restoration – restoring and protecting the colonists' customary rights as Englishmen – as the goal.

But like any great historical event, the American Revolution was complicated, with many aspects. Even those fighting on the same side sometimes saw the cause differently. In fact, to a greater extent than many of us appreciate today, the Revolutionary War took on many of the aspects of a civil war, pitting Loyalists against Patriots, dividing families and towns and regions and social classes against one another. It led to fierce struggles over fundamental political and social values.

Loyalty to the Crown had been the automatic response of a sizable minority of Americans. But the resonant words of the Declaration of Independence pointed toward a larger aspiration, something more than mere restoration. They pointed toward the emergence on the world stage of something genuinely new: a republican order of self-rule built on a commitment to equality and liberty.

Historians still argue about the best way to think about the Revolution. Was the Revolution essentially conservative in its objectives? Was it merely seeking to separate America from Britain in order to return things to the way they had been before the unacceptable new British colonial policies? Or was it something more radical, shaking things up dramatically, not merely changing the names and faces of those at the top? Was it true, as one historian has said, that "the war was not about home rule, but about who would rule at home"?

There is some evidence for that last claim. Certainly the war strengthened some radical currents that had been operating in society for many decades. Think back to how the Great Awakening had weakened the authority of established clergymen, while unleashing a sense of individualism and self-reliance and willingness to question authority throughout the culture. In the same way, the war against British colonial rule had placed all forms of settled authority under suspicion, including the homegrown class distinctions that were a fairly settled part of colonial life. Once a revolution starts, it can be hard to stop, even when it goes far beyond its initial goals.

The American Revolution was not just a matter of lawyers and other well-off people. It had drawn upon the enthusiasm and energy of laborers, farmers, mechanics, servants, and common people of every type to start demonstrations, support boycotts, and fight battles that ultimately made independence possible. Didn't they deserve some share of the triumph? How could all this idealistic talk of liberty and equality not call into question the right of the wealthy and wellborn to rule?

And how could it not ultimately call into question the existence in the new nation of an institution that most glaringly stood in contradiction to self-rule, liberty, and equality: the institution of chattel slavery?

Such questions could not be easily set aside. But the immediate task at hand was to devise a working government. The newly independent Americans were determined to get along without a monarch and to uphold the possibility of republican self-rule. But how to do it?

Those among the Founding generation who knew about the history of previous republics, especially those in classical antiquity, knew that the single most common characteristic of a republic was its fragility. Everything depended upon the virtuous character of the citizenry, on their willingness to live as George Washington had done and place the well-being of the public over and above their own personal interests. Such civic virtue was rare and hard to sustain in a whole society.

The size and scale of a republic also mattered. Philosophers such as Aristotle and Montesquieu had said that a republic had to be small if it was to maintain itself as a republic. Large nations tended either to fall apart into discord or to be transformed into empires under kings or emperors. The historical example of Rome haunted the early Americans for that very reason. The Roman Republic had become strong through the civic virtues of its hardy citizenry. The Roman Empire had fallen into ruin because of the decadence and corruption of its inhabitants. Many Americans feared that Great Britain in the age of George III was following that same downward path. They wanted to spare themselves that fate.

Hence the emphasis on American constitution making, starting in 1776, would first be on the state level. Most everyone agreed that the states should continue to be the main sources of political power and authority. They were the chief protectors of individual rights and guardians against abuses of power. Generally, this meant limiting the power of governors and giving more of it to legislatures. It most certainly meant reserving for the national government *only* the most essential elements of power.

In fact, there hadn't even been a national constitution properly in place during most of the war years. The Articles of Confederation, which were the nation's first effort at a constitution, had been drafted in 1777 but were not ratified by all the states until 1781. It mattered very little, though. The Continental Congress had already been operating as if the Articles were in place anyway, so their formal adoption didn't change much.

What did the Articles look like? Remember, the Declaration of Independence had almost nothing to say about the shape that a union of "free and independent states" would take. But an examination of the Articles sheds some light on the matter. The Articles understood the combination of states as a "league of friendship" rather than a firm union, let alone a combination of the states into some larger whole. The states were to be of *primary* importance. Article II specified that "each state retains its sovereignty, freedom, and independence, and every Power, Jurisdiction, and right, which is not by this confederation expressly delegated to the United States, in Congress assembled." Each state, whether large or small, would have a single vote in Congress, and for the passage of the most important measures (things having to do with currency, tariffs, or the military), either a unanimous vote or a two-thirds supermajority was required. And the national government was not to be given any coercive tools – no courts, no executive power, no power of taxation – that would allow it to act independently or to force the individual states to do anything they didn't want to do.

In retrospect, it's easy to see why the Articles' approach was unlikely to succeed. But it also is important to try to understand why the revolutionary generation overwhelmingly favored it at first.

For one thing, the war itself was still under way in the 1770s and early 1780s, and there was simply no time to debate a dramatic change in the form of government. But there was a far deeper reason. The leaders of the day were influenced by their own immediate history. None of them wanted to create the same problems of an overly powerful government that they had just overthrown. That outcome was to be avoided at all costs. But this anxiety blinded the framers of the Articles to the other issues that a new government would have to confront if it were to be effective. They overreacted, going too far in the opposite direction, and created for themselves a weak and unworkable central government: one that avoided centralization, yes, but to such an extent that it couldn't do the jobs that needed doing. It could neither conduct foreign policy nor regulate interstate trade nor defend the nation's borders nor put the nation's economic and financial house in order.

Before taking note of these failings, though, we must take note of one major exception, a very impressive and enduring accomplishment of the Congress under the Articles. That was the establishment of wise and farsighted policies for the development of western lands, formulated in the great Northwest Ordinance of 1787. These laws laid down the procedures by which the western territories could be settled, organized, and incorporated into the nation, in a way that not only extended fundamental American principles and promoted stability but also generated revenue for the national treasury.

The Northwest Ordinance provided a clearly defined process by which the western lands would, in several stages, eventually be "formed into distinct republican States." The historian Daniel Boorstin called it "the add-a-state plan." It ensured that the western lands would not be held as permanent colonial dependencies but would gradually enter the Union on terms exactly equal to that of the already existing states. This was no small thing!

The result would be a steadily growing country, not an empire, and a country with a growing spirit of unity. And that was not all. The Ordinance also prohibited the introduction of slavery into the territory and took a strong stand in favor of educational institutions, setting aside public lands for that purpose. "Religion, morality and knowledge being necessary to good government and the happiness of mankind," it stated, "schools and the means of education shall forever be encouraged."

These were real achievements. But in most other respects, the nation's interests were poorly served by the Articles. In the western frontier areas, the British refused to withdraw from the several military posts that they had established, even though the terms of the

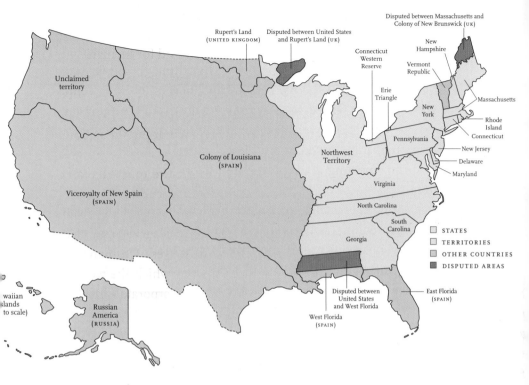

States and territories of the United States in 1790, including the Northwest Territory.

Treaty of Paris had required it. Who was going to force them out? In the Southwest, the Spanish similarly refused to yield control over the Mississippi River, the commercial lifeline to the country's mid-section. Such actions were a poke in the eye of the Americans, who simply lacked the means to respond effectively to them.

But that was not all. The British succeeded in badly damaging the American economy by severely restricting American imports and flooding American markets with their own low-priced manufactured goods. This wave of British economic pressure came as the United States was already reeling from a postwar economic depression. The result was that debtors, especially farmers, suddenly found themselves without enough income to meet their obligations, including paying the mortgages on their properties. Lenders began to take back debtors' property, in the legal process called foreclosure, and to push farmers off their land.

Debtors pleaded for relief in the form of extending credit and printing more and more paper money. Unfortunately, these were exactly the things that the bankers and politicians felt they could not do, since they feared such actions would make the economy even worse. Conditions were ripe for an eruption. In several places, desperate mobs attempted to stop foreclosures by force, blocking courts from meeting and preventing them from doing their business.

Such conflicts escalated to an alarming level of conflict between debtors and creditors, between haves and have-nots. The state governments were levying ever-higher taxes, trying their best to pay off the massive debts they had accumulated in the conduct of the war. But there was a sense of injustice in it all. Many of the holders of that debt were wealthy men living comfortably in places like Boston. Many of the debtors were struggling farmers who had fought in the war and returned to find their livelihoods and their homes in peril.

One particularly notable uprising took place in western Massachusetts in summer 1786, when Revolutionary War veteran Daniel Shays led a march on Springfield to shut down the state supreme court and then attack the Springfield arsenal. Although the incident died down quickly and had little lasting effect in Massachusetts, it was widely noticed by some of the nation's leaders, who saw it as an alarming indication that the liberatory energies released by the war were starting to run riot. George Washington worried that the country was "fast verging to anarchy and confusion!"

The deficiencies of the Articles had long been apparent. The importance of Shays' Rebellion was in clarifying that perception and imparting a sense of urgency to the task of reform. Even as Washington wrote, plans were afoot, spurred by Washington's brilliant young aide Alexander Hamilton, to gather "a Convention of Deputies from the different States, for the special and sole purpose of [devising] a plan for supplying such defects as may be discovered to exist" in the Articles. That convention would finally gather in Philadelphia on May 25, 1787. Nearly four months later, on September 17, it would emerge having produced an entirely new Constitution for the United States. The Constitution that it framed (which is why we call the convention delegates "the Framers") has endured as the nation's fundamental law even to the present day and become the oldest written constitution in human history. What is the secret of its success? Read on to find out.

8 · MAKING A CONSTITUTION

THE HIGH CALIBER of the men who represented the respective states in Philadelphia was staggering, particularly given how young they were, with an average age of forty-two. Some older men were present – George Washington (fifty-five) himself was elected to preside over the convention, Roger Sherman of Connecticut (sixty-six) played a major role in the debates, and Benjamin Franklin, then a spritely eighty-one, worked behind the scenes. But most of the work was done by a handful of delegates under the age of fifty, men such as James Wilson of Pennsylvania (forty-two), Gouverneur Morris of New York (thirty-five), and, perhaps most important of all, James Madison of Virginia (thirty-six). He was by all accounts the central figure of the convention and was the principal architect of the Constitution itself.

Unlike the tall and muscular Washington, Madison did not look the heroic part he was given by history to play. His nickname was "Little Jemmy" because he was such a tiny, frail man. He stood a mere five feet four inches tall, weighed only one hundred pounds, and had a squeaky voice and a reticent, bookish manner. But no one doubted his high intelligence, his knowledge of history, and his eloquence and persuasiveness in debate.

His intelligence combined the experience of a practical politician with the thoughtfulness of a philosopher. His knowledge of the past gave him a keen appreciation of the possibilities within America's grasp. He intended that America should make the most of those possibilities. Getting the Constitution right would be a high-stakes affair. America, he asserted, would "decide for ever the fate of republican government."

Such weighty words reflected the Framers' remarkable combination of soaring ambition and practical humility. They were excited by the possibilities that lay before them and felt a determination to lay hold of them. As John Adams said, they were living in a time in which "the greatest lawgivers of antiquity would have wished to live," with a chance to establish "the wisest and happiest government that human wisdom can contrive." Hence they quickly decided to expand their mission beyond the narrow one of merely correcting the Articles. Instead, they would create something far better, something that could be an example to the world.

But their large ambitions were always tempered by realism. They were careful, always mindful of the ominous example of Rome, always aware of the frailty and imperfection of human nature. The best constitution would be one built with both the best and the worst aspects of human nature firmly in mind.

The debates that emerged at the Philadelphia convention would often revolve around the differing interests of the various states. But there also was a great deal of agreement about certain fundamental principles.

There was agreement that the new government should continue to be republican, meaning that it would rule out the possibility of any kind of monarch or monarchical office.

There was agreement on the basic principle, worked out in the political turmoil of seventeenth-century England, that power should never be concentrated in any one person or office but should be divided and spread out as widely as possible: in a Parliament, in state and local governments, in common law and tradition, and in the strong belief that every person possessed certain fundamental liberties and rights that no government could violate. The delegates agreed that the chief challenge of constitution making was to ensure that these different sources of power were so arranged that they could check and balance one another, ensuring that even with a more powerful national government, no one branch, faction, or region would dominate the others.

The delegates favored a *federal* system. We should be sure we understand what that word means. For us today, the term *federal* immediately makes us think of a powerful national government. But it meant something very different to the Framers. It meant a system that would maintain a large degree of independence for the states, while turning over to a national government only those things that had to be undertaken in common. Ideally, this federal system would combine the advantages of self-rule with the advantages of union, the diversity of smaller-scale local organization with the powers of a unified national state. It would be a difficult balance to strike, though, and even more difficult to hold. It was one thing to say it, another thing to do it.

In a sense, the history of the British Empire to that date had already demonstrated how difficult such a "federal" reconciliation would be, particularly in the absence of a written constitution to spell out how power was to be distributed through the imperial system. Consider the bitterly divisive question of taxation for the colonies. That problem could not be solved so long as there was no shared understanding of how the pieces of the empire would fit together, how they could be part of a larger whole, while holding on to their right of self-rule. Might a more creative brand of leadership in Great Britain and America have come up with a federal understanding of the British Empire that could have kept the empire intact? It seems unlikely, but who knows?

In any event, the Philadelphia convention would have to address itself to very similar questions and incorporate its answers into the document the delegates were drafting. After electing George Washington to preside over the convention, and voting to close the proceedings and meet in secret, the delegates faced two fundamental decisions: How much power needed to be given to an expanded national government? How could they make sure that this empowered national government would itself be fully accountable, would not become *too* powerful?

The convention was held in secrecy. But thanks to Madison's notes on the proceedings, we know a great deal about how things went. Early on, the delegates agreed that the Articles had to be scrapped completely. They also agreed readily on most of the new powers that would be granted to the national government: the right to levy taxes, regulate interstate and foreign commerce, raise and maintain the army and navy, call up the state militias, regulate currency, negotiate treaties, and impose tariffs.

The powerful new office of the presidency represented the most striking departure from the decentralized Articles. One may well wonder whether the delegates would ever have been willing to take a chance on such a dramatically expanded office had George Washington not been available to fill the position. Once again, Washington showed himself to be the essential man.

Even so, the leap of faith being made, and asked for, was considerable. The president would have responsibility for executing the laws and directing the foreign policy of the nation. He would serve as commander in chief of the armed forces. He would appoint federal judges and secretaries of executive branch agencies. He would have the power to veto congressional legislation, and his veto could only be overridden by a supermajority of two-thirds. There was no precedent for this in the colonial experience – aside, that is, from the figure of the king.

But the main debates emerged over other issues, particularly the question of how representation in Congress would be determined. Two competing approaches were under consideration. Madison's initial plan, which came to be called the Virginia Plan, called for representation by population. The smaller states, which rightly feared that this arrangement would make them second-class citizens under the new Constitution, fought back and, under the leadership of William Paterson, proposed what came to be called the New Jersey Plan, which would maintain the Articles' pattern of representation by states.

This clash was a question not only of contending interests but of competing principles. Representation by state, in which each state had equal representation, seemed to violate the very principle of democracy itself, rendering the votes of those in the populous states less valuable than those in the small states. Why should tiny Rhode Island have the same legislative power as large and populous Virginia? But representation by population had its problems, too, for it violated the principle that the country was, as its name implies, a union of *states*, in which the states remained the fundamental unit upon which the nation was built. The Framers had no intention of giving up that principle.

The Convention eventually settled on a compromise between these two positions. This Great Compromise was, like all such compromises, a political deal. But it ended up being something much more than that. Instead of favoring one principle over another, it acknowledged the legitimate aspects of *both* principles, giving both their due and putting them into fruitful tension with one another. The key was the use of a bicameral or two-house structure, patterned after the British division of Parliament into a House of Commons and an aristocratic House of Lords. In the American version, representation by population would be the rule in the House of Representatives, while in the Senate, the upper house, each state would be granted two senators, whatever its size or population might be.

Legislation would have to clear both of these very different houses, with their different principles of representation, and be signed by the president to be enacted into law. The interests of conflicting groups could thereby all have a role in determining the fate of important legislation. The House of Representatives would be closer to the great mass of ordinary citizens and chosen by popular vote for short, two-year terms. The Senate was designed to be more aristocratic and somewhat shielded from the winds of popular sentiment, with its members elected for six-year terms by the state legislatures rather than by the people at large. The House would be entrusted with the sole power of introducing tax bills; the Senate would handle foreign relations, the ratification of treaties, and confirmation of executive branch appointments.

The result of this compromise was a structure that was better than either of the alternatives. It became one of the chief elements in the Constitution's intricate network of checks and balances, a system designed to make sure that each power granted to one part of the government is kept within safe limits by opposing powers assigned to some other part.

This pattern played out on multiple levels. The newly established national government would have greater powers, but its powers would be *enumerated*, meaning that they are counted out, and thereby limited by the Constitution itself, and by the state governments, which would remain strong, serving as an additional check.

The national government was further checked by being subdivided into executive, legislative, and judicial branches, each of which had some ways of thwarting the others in cases of bad judgment or overreach. The president could reject a bill of Congress with a veto. Congress could override that veto by repassing the bill with a two-thirds majority. Congress could remove the president and members of the executive branch through impeachment. The Senate could reject executive branch appointments. The president could command the armed forces and negotiate treaties, but only the Congress could declare war, and only the Senate could ratify treaties. And so on.

Behind all these particulars was a powerful idea. Conflict is part of human nature and can never be eliminated; neither can the desire for power and the tendency of flawed human beings to abuse it. Therefore a good constitution has to provide a structure within which conflict can be channeled and the search for power can be kept within bounds. Think of it as being like an internal combustion engine. Such a constitution is designed to control the energies released by the explosions that take place within its chambers, and to use those energies to drive the work of American governance and enterprise.

Or to put it another way, it should be designed to work with the grain of human nature, and not against it; but in doing so, it should also counteract the worst tendencies of human nature, rather than encourage them. The only thing all contending parties need to agree on is the authority of the Constitution itself and the rules of engagement it sets forth.

9 · SUCCESS,
AND AN AWFUL PRICE

So THIS WAS the document that the delegates agreed on in Philadelphia and signed on September 17, 1787. Let's pause here for a moment to step back and reflect on the larger picture. Constitution Day, which we observe every September 17, is a singularly American holiday, even more unique than the Fourth of July. After all, many nations have their great leaders and laborers, their war heroes, their monuments, and their days of independence. But there is only one nation on earth that can point with pride to a written Constitution that is more than 230 years old, an expression of fundamental law that stands at the very center of our national life.

As such, the U.S. Constitution is not merely our most important legal document; it is an expression of who and what we are. Other countries, such as France, have lived under many different constitutions and kinds of government over the centuries. The idea of "France" is something separable from the form of government that happens to be in power at any given time. It's not so for Americans, who have lived since the 1780s under one regime, a remarkable fact whose significance nevertheless seems to escape us. Yes, we do revere our Constitution, but we do so blandly and automatically, without troubling ourselves to know very much about it and without reflecting much about what our Constitution says about our national identity.

That identity is a complicated one, and there are elements of it about which we all will probably never agree. Ties of blood and religion and race and soil are not enough to hold us together as Americans. They never have been. We think of "diversity" as something new in American history, but in fact, American life has always involved dealing with profound differences among us. Our Constitution accepted the inevitability of our diversity and the inevitability of conflicts arising out of our differences. In addition, it recognized the fact that ambitious, covetous, and power-hungry individuals are always going to be among us and that the energies of such potentially dangerous people need to be contained and tamed, diverted into activities that promote and protect the public good.

Hence we have a Constitution that is not filled with soaring rhetoric or lists of high-sounding principles. It is instead a dry and functional document laying out a complex system of rules, careful divisions of function and power that provide the means by which conflicts can be both expressed and contained. Unlike the Declaration of Independence, its spirit is unspoken; that spirit would be revealed not through words but through events that would express the unfolding demands of history.

That history has been largely successful – yet not entirely so. There was one important respect in which the Constitution they wrote fell short, and grievously so. And that was in its failure to address the growing national stain of slavery. As we will see, there were understandable reasons for that omission. But the trajectory of history that was coming would not forget it, and would not forgive it.

Slavery is as old as human history, and its existence has sadly been more the rule than the exception in that history. It already existed in the New World, even before Columbus arrived, along with even worse practices, such as cannibalism and human sacrifice. Its introduction by Europeans was pioneered by the Portuguese and Spanish, beginning in the sixteenth century and only later picked up by the English. It was not a part of any larger plan for British colonization, and it did not take root immediately in colonial North

America – although the forced-labor system known as indentured servitude was common in the British colonies from the start, and it could be said to resemble slavery in its harshness and cruelty. In fact, indentured servitude was so common that some historians have estimated that more than half of the white immigrants to the American colonies up to the time of the Revolution had come to the New World under indentures.

Although often a brutal institution, indentured servitude served a real economic purpose. The colonies were desperately in need of a steady supply of laborers, especially in the agricultural areas near the Chesapeake, which suffered from a high mortality rate due to disease, food shortages, and constant Indian conflicts. But a great many desperately poor Europeans who were otherwise willing to come to America and endure such severe conditions didn't have the money to pay for their own voyage. Indentured servitude allowed them to solve that problem, temporarily trading their freedom for the cost of their passage, signing contracts lasting from four to seven years with masters or landowners who would pay for their transportation and upkeep in exchange for their work, usually on a farm. At the termination of their contracts, they would be free to go their own way, working for wages or acquiring their own land.

The first Africans enjoyed the same conditions as the whites, and the African population grew slowly, to about four hundred laborers by 1650. But as it grew, so, too, did the practice of discrimination against Africans on account of their race. By the 1660s, such practices had hardened into laws enacted by colonial assemblies, which dictated that Africans and their offspring were to be kept in permanent bondage. The Africans were being made into chattel slaves, the legal property of their owners.

The use of slavery began to grow as the agricultural economy grew, and as an improving British economy meant that the flow of white indentured servants from England slowed sharply. Little by little, the cheap and dependable labor supplied by slavery became an essential part of the agricultural economy in states like Virginia and South Carolina. By 1750, half the population of Virginia and two-thirds of South Carolina was enslaved. Yet it should be remembered that slavery was not exclusively a southern practice; at the time of the Revolution, every state in the union permitted it.

By the time of the Constitutional Convention, the institution of race-based slavery was deeply enmeshed in the national economy, despite all the ways that its very existence stood in glaring contradiction to the national commitment to equality and self-rule. Hence there was real bite to the mocking question fired at the Americans in 1775 by the British writer Samuel Johnson: "How is it that we hear the loudest yelps for liberty among the drivers of negroes?"

It was an excellent question, particularly if one kept in mind how many of the most prominent Founders, including Thomas Jefferson and George Washington, were themselves owners of slaves. How, we wonder today, could such otherwise enlightened and admirable men and women have been so blind to the fundamental humanity of those they confined? How could they have made their peace with practices so utterly contradictory to all they stood for?

There is no easy answer to such questions. But surely a part of the answer is that each of us is born into a world that we did not make, and it is only with the greatest effort, and often at very great cost, that we are ever able to change that world for the better. Moral sensibilities are not fixed; they develop and deepen over time, and general moral progress is very slow. Part of the study of history involves a training of the imagination, learning to see historical actors as speaking and acting in their own times rather than ours and learning to see even our heroes as an all-too-human mixture of admirable and unadmirable qualities, people like us who may, like us, struggle with circumstances beyond their control.

Yet something more needs to be said. As Johnson understood, what made the American situation especially intolerable was not the wrongs these earliest Americans practiced but the high ideals that they professed, ideals that served to condemn those very practices. They were living an inconsistency, and they could not be at ease about it. Washington freed his own slaves upon his death. Jefferson did not, but he opposed slavery, agonized over his involvement with it, and later in life saw slavery as an offense against God and a possible source of national breakup. The seeds of a better understanding had been planted and begun to take root, but they were not yet ready to blossom.

It is also true that many of the Framers sincerely believed that slavery was already on the way out and would eventually disappear. They therefore were willing to accept the compromises in the Constitution for the sake of a brighter future of whose coming they were very confident. Roger Sherman observed that "the abolition of slavery seemed to be going on in the United States, and that the good sense of the several States would probably by degrees complete it." Similarly, his fellow Connecticut delegate Oliver Ellsworth predicted that "Slavery, in time, will not be a speck in our Country."

The results of the Convention reflected this mixed and uncertain condition. Sadly, little serious consideration was given to the idea of abolishing slavery at the time. Indeed, some delegates were bound by their states' economic interests to oppose any measure that would even disfavor slavery. One delegate from South Carolina threatened that his delegation and the Georgia delegation would never agree to a Constitution that failed to protect slavery. In other words, the price of pursuing abolition of slavery at that time would almost certainly have been the falling apart of the American nation, which would probably have rendered the resulting nation-fragments highly unstable and unable to defend their interests. Would that have been worth the price? That is a much easier question for us to ask today than it was for them to answer at the time.

In any event, the defenders of slavery got their way and also gained a concession, through an idea carried over from a proposed amendment to the Articles: that three-fifths of the slave population would be counted for representation and taxation purposes, even though slaves had none of the rights of citizens. (Northern delegates had wanted slaves to be counted at 100 percent for taxation purposes but at zero for representation purposes; they were forced to compromise.) They also got a concession protecting the transatlantic slave trade until 1808 and a fugitive slave clause, which required that a "person held to service or labour" (a term that could include indentured servants) who escapes to another state must be "delivered up" to the owner or master to whom the person's service was due.

So slavery would be protected. But the Constitution was otherwise notably silent on the subject. Note, for example, the unwillingness, in the Fugitive Slave Clause, to use the word "owner" or "master." The word "slavery" never appears in the Constitution's text. The Framers showed by their silence that they were not at ease with slavery and preferred softer words such as "persons held to Service or labour" to the more direct "slaves." It is important that the Constitution nowhere endorsed the idea that there is a property right in human beings. Madison made sure of that.

It is also indicative that the final document did open the way to an ending of the transatlantic slave trade after the year 1808, a move inspired by a resounding speech from George Mason of Virginia. Mason was himself a slaveholder, but he was also a Christian who labeled the trade an "infernal traffic" and feared the corrupting spread of slavery through the entire nation, which would bring "the judgment of Heaven" down severely upon any country in which bondage was widespread and blandly accepted. His own state of Virginia had been one of the first places in the world to stop the importation of slaves for sale, doing so in 1778 under the leadership of its governor, Thomas Jefferson. These things say a lot about the Framers' conflicted hearts.

The legal importation of African slaves into the United States did end in 1808, under the leadership of then-president Thomas Jefferson. But slavery itself persisted and grew in the American South, since the conditions of life in the United States would prove favorable to a steady natural increase in the slave population (in contrast to the sugar islands of the West Indies or the cane fields of Brazil).

So it was an imperfect Constitution. Inconsistencies regarding slavery were inherent in its structure. These inconsistencies were almost certainly unavoidable in the short term to achieve an effective political union of the nation. But if this inconsistency was a political necessity, it was a moral tragedy, with effects that would persist for nearly a century to come, in ways that would eventually leave the nation wounded and scarred.

Even so, it would be profoundly wrong to contend, as some do, that the United States was "founded on" slavery. No, it was *founded* on other principles entirely, on principles of liberty and self-rule that had been discovered and refined through several turbulent centuries of European and British and American history. Those foundational principles would win out in the end, though not without much struggle and striving, and eventual bloodshed.

We live today on the other side of a great transformation in moral awareness, a transformation that was taking place, but was not yet completed, in the very years that the United States was being formed. The United States enjoyed a miraculous birth, but it was not the product of a perfect delivery. Few things in this life are.

10 · NEW BEGINNINGS

The new U.S. Constitution had now been drafted and approved by the Philadelphia Convention. But it still would have to be approved by the states, in a process called ratification, before it could become the supreme law of the land. The Framers knew that achieving this goal was not going to be easy or certain. A great many Americans were not yet on board with the idea of changing things, especially if it meant a great expansion of national power. Their reluctance was not just a matter of principle; it also was sometimes a matter of their self-interest. Local authorities feared being overruled by national ones; state legislatures looked with suspicion on any new national constitution that would reduce their powers.

The Framers knew there would be such obstacles, and they wanted the new charter to get the strongest possible endorsement from the people. So they declared in Article VII that this Constitution would become law automatically upon ratification by conventions from nine of the thirteen states. The idea of using "conventions" was brilliant. By requiring that the ratification be done through state conventions created for the occasion, rather than the existing state legislatures, the process could work around the existing officials, who would be the very ones especially resistant to change.

But in every state would be heated debates. Supporters of the new constitution, who called themselves "Federalists," faced opponents with the awkward name "Anti-Federalists." The Anti-Federalists wanted to keep the loose and decentralized approach of the Articles and distrusted the Constitution's concentration of power in the national government, especially the presidency.

We can make a few generalizations about the people on either side. The Federalists, many of whose leaders had participated in the Philadelphia Convention, were likely to be well-off professional people, knowledgeable, organized, and adept at producing the kind of sophisticated arguments and publicity that could sway delegates to vote their way. The Anti-Federalists were a more varied group. Although a few were quite wealthy, many others were small farmers and debtors of modest means.

In any event, the issue was very much in doubt. No one could know for sure which side would prevail. The Critical Period was not over yet.

The Federalist versus Anti-Federalist debates were an example of a tension, one we have already seen before, between those who favored a strong central government and those who distrusted all forms of centralized power. This division would run through many of the conflicts in the American nation's early history, from the Anglo-American imperial conflicts of the 1760s through the early years of the nineteenth century and beyond, even to the present day. Both sides had a good case to make, with proven patriots making strong arguments. In many states, the convention votes would be very close.

The debates over the Constitution stimulated Americans to think hard about their political principles, and they gave rise to an abundance of spirited and thoughtful writings on both sides: pamphlets, editorials, and newspaper articles. The authors often disguised their identities behind Roman pen names like Brutus and Cato. But the discussion was nearly always on a very high level, staying away from personalities, and instead offering real insight into the issues at hand. It was a great process of public self-education.

Probably the most important of these writings were the eighty-five articles written in support of ratification by three of the Constitution's chief backers: Alexander Hamilton, James Madison, and John Jay. These fascinating essays were thoughtful and knowledgeable, in ways that reflected the Founding generation's remarkable combination of intellectual maturity and political savvy. Amazingly, the essays were published in the New York newspapers, appearing under the pen name of Publius. The collection of all eighty-five essays into a single volume has been known ever after as *The Federalist* or *The Federalist Papers*. It became an instant classic and is still regarded today as the single best guide to the Framers' understanding of the Constitution.

Many of the papers in *The Federalist* showed original thinking and went on to become important contributions to the history of political thought. That is pretty unusual for newspaper columns. In *Federalist* 10, for example, James Madison put forward a brilliant discussion of the problem of factions – opposing groups – in political life, exploring where they come from and how they can be controlled. He showed how a large and diverse republic like the United States could solve the factionalism to which small republics are prone. In *Federalist* 51, he put forward an explanation of how the Constitution's federal system provided a "double security" for the rights of the people, by pitting the states against the national government and dividing the national government against itself.

Beneath it all was a very realistic view of human beings. "Ambition must be made to counteract ambition," Madison warned, because although a society needed the energy of its ambitious men, the most ambitious men were likely also to be the worst if they became corrupt. You couldn't depend on the goodness of human nature to prevail if you wanted a stable government. No one was above factional strife, because the causes of faction were "sown into the nature of man."

But perhaps the most important statement offered in the *Federalist* was written by Hamilton and appeared at the beginning of *Federalist* 1. It showed just how seriously the Framers took their task:

> *It has been frequently remarked that it seems to have been reserved to the people of this country, by their conduct and example, to decide the important question, whether societies of men are really capable or not of establishing good government from reflection and choice, or whether they are forever destined to depend for their political constitutions on*

accident and force. If there be any truth in the remark, the crisis at which we are arrived may with propriety be regarded as the era in which that decision is to be made; and a wrong election of the part we shall act may, in this view, deserve to be considered as the general misfortune of mankind.

The advocates of the new Constitution believed in their cause, because they believed the stakes were very high. They believed that their fight for a good and effective constitution, one that was created not by the collision of brute forces but by calm and patient reason, was an effort on behalf not only of the American people but of the whole world.

Although Hamilton was not a deeply religious man, he was echoing the Puritan idea of "commission," of a responsibility both grand and solemn. But he gave it a different twist, because the Federalists were doing something quite different from what John Winthrop had sought to do. They were not founding a Zion in the wilderness. They were creating a structure of secular government, a charter of fundamental law that would support the ideals of liberty and self-rule. They were using reflection and choice to engage in one of the great experiments in the annals of politics, attempting to use the example of previous republics to avert those republics' fate. They were using history to defy history.

The ratification debates are well worth studying in great detail. But the Federalists were able to win in the end, even winning ratification in the difficult and contentious state of New York. But the Anti-Federalists, despite their defeat and their awkward name, had a voice worth hearing and deserve more credit than they generally get. For they made a vital contribution to the eventual shape of the nation.

They had feared, with reason, that a more powerful central government might turn out to be tyrannical and might abuse the rights and liberties for which Americans had fought their Revolution. No one expressed that fear more memorably than the revolutionary hero Patrick Henry, who rose to speak against the Constitution at the Virginia State Ratifying Convention, calling it a document that "squints toward monarchy," aiming to make the country "a great and mighty empire" whose passion for grandeur and vainglory would prove "incompatible with the genius of republicanism."

Many Virginians preferred the republican simplicity of farming life, and Henry's powerful words touched the deep anxieties in them. That anxiety convinced them and many other Americans of the need for a bill of rights to protect fundamental liberties. In response to these legitimate fears, the victorious Federalists promised to make the necessary adjustments to the Constitution as one of the first acts of the new government.

They were true to their word, and the result was the first ten amendments to the Constitution, which have ever thereafter come to be regarded as an essential part of it. These were passed almost immediately by the First Congress and adopted by the states in 1791, with the goal of guaranteeing that the new Congress would make no laws infringing upon such rights as the freedom of religion, freedom of speech and the press, the right to bear arms, the right to a trial by jury, protection against unreasonable search and seizure, protection against the requirement to offer self-incriminating testimony, protection of due process rights, and other similar rights. In addition, the Tenth Amendment provided that any rights not explicitly given to the national government remained in the hands of the states or individuals.

The adoption of the Bill of Rights calmed all but the most determined critics of the Constitution. And although Madison and others had thought such a bill of rights was unnecessary, history has shown them to be quite wrong about that. The Anti-Federalists were not wrong about a great many of their concerns. Few of us today would ever want to see the Constitution stripped of, say, its First Amendment, which guarantees freedom of religion, freedom of speech, and freedom of the press.

In fact, the Bill of Rights has become one of the glories of the American constitutional system and, despite its added-on status, is seen by many as the very heart of the Constitution. It is one of the ironies of history that some of the fiercest opponents of the Constitution turned out to be among its chief benefactors – although maybe that was not as ironic as it might seem, since the Constitution itself was designed as an instrument to harness the energies of disagreeing factions and groups. Remember, the Framers themselves incorporated their own quarrels into a Constitution that was in many ways better than what either side would have sought on its own. The ratification process did the same thing.

But many skeptics at the time were not convinced that the Constitution could last very long. Even George Washington confided to one of his fellow delegates that he did not expect it to last more than twenty years. He would have been as shocked as anyone to find it still functioning more than 234 years later.

His pessimism had a basis in reality, though. The Constitution was a remarkable achievement and a beacon of hope. But it was also very much an experiment. It was a rough outline rather than a detailed plan, an architect's rendering rather than a finished building. No one could know for sure whether it would work. It had an elaborate system of checks and balances, but who could know for sure what would happen when they were put to the test? It laid down some of the procedures by which decisions were made, but it offered little guidance as to what the content of those decisions should be. It featured a powerful presidency but offered little insight into how and where the president ought to exercise that power.

You could compare the Constitution to a musical composition. As of early 1789, it was nothing more than sheet music, elaborate notes written on paper. It was artfully done, perhaps, but meaningless until translated into actual sounds – and no one yet knew exactly what it would actually sound like, or whether there would be musicians skillful enough to play the music properly. So many things remained to be filled in, connected – and fought over.

It made all the difference, though, that the dignified and universally trusted figure of George Washington would be available to serve as the first president. It had been in fact assumed by many at the Convention that he would be the one to hold that office. Sure enough, when the ballots of the first presidential electors were counted in the Senate on April 6, 1789, Washington was unanimously elected. On April 30, he took the oath of office at Federal Hall on Wall Street in New York City, which would be the seat of the national government for the next year.

In his inaugural address delivered in the Senate chamber that day, Washington clearly and crisply echoed the vision that Hamilton had put forward in *Federalist* 1: "The preservation of the sacred fire of liberty, and the destiny of the Republican model of Government, are justly considered as deeply, perhaps as finally staked, on the experiment entrusted to the hands of the American people." The very future of liberty and self-rule: the stakes of the American experiment would be nothing less.

Truth be told, though, Washington did not want the job. Even observers at his inauguration noted a certain hesitancy in his manner and modesty in his words, notwithstanding the military bearing of his tall, impressive figure and the ceremonial army sword he held. Nearing the age of sixty, after enduring two grinding decades of war and politics in which he always found himself thrust into a central role in determining the direction of his country, he was tired. He wanted nothing so much as to be free of those burdens – to retire from public life and return to Virginia, where he could enjoy the private joys of a gentleman farmer at his beautiful Mount Vernon.

But that was not yet to be. Washington was blessed and cursed with a destiny – the destiny of being America's "indispensable man," as his biographer James Thomas Flexner rightly called him. He was the natural leader to whom everyone looked again and again for wisdom, impartiality, and his ability to inspire the nation. His duty was clear. If the task before the country was a great experiment on behalf of all humanity but entrusted to the American people – an experiment that, like all experiments, could fail – how could he refuse? Particularly when he knew that he could do the job better than anyone else, at the nation's hour of need.

His enormous sense of personal responsibility also made him very self-aware. He knew that every decision he made and every action he took would have consequences, and this made him uncomfortable. "The eyes of Argus," the mythical giant of a hundred eyes, "are upon me," he complained, "and no slip will pass unnoticed." He told his friend Madison that "everything in our situation will serve to establish a Precedent," and for that reason, "it is devoutly wished on my part, that these precedents may be fixed on true principles."

And so they were. Every one of his actions was carefully thought through, from his cautiously distant relations with Congress to his scrupulous avoidance of any hint of favoritism in his appointments to his extreme care to project the right kind of public image, with a dignified and tasteful majesty untainted by excess – the sort of image that he thought appropriate to the republican leader of a great country.

One thing was certain – the whole world *would* be watching.

11 · THE WASHINGTON ADMINISTRATION

WASHINGTON'S LEADERSHIP STYLE affected the choices he made for his executive branch appointments. These men were chosen for their general ability and loyalty, and not for their political connections. Like so many military men, Washington intensely disliked political parties, and like so many of the Framers, he hoped that the new nation could avoid having them altogether.

Following that pattern, he picked an impressive but diverse cabinet: Thomas Jefferson of Virginia as secretary of state, Alexander Hamilton of New York as secretary of the Treasury, General Henry Knox of Massachusetts as secretary of war, and Edmund Randolph of Virginia as attorney general. He also established the precedent, not mentioned in the Constitution, of bringing these advisors together as a "cabinet," for the purpose of offering general advice to him, even outside their assigned areas.

The most urgent problem his administration faced was the country's perilous financial state. Treasury secretary Hamilton, a brilliant and forward-thinking leader with great energy and a firm commitment to the ideal of national greatness, addressed those problems head-on. Hamilton was a self-made man who had risen from a lowly birth on a Caribbean island to become Washington's personal aide during the Revolutionary War, and then one of the most successful lawyers in New York, as well as a skillful political operator.

Hamilton was deeply involved in the campaign for a new Constitution, and he had vast ambitions for the American economy.

America, he enthused, was a "Hercules in the cradle" that would soon have a booming economy if it did the right things. To that end, Hamilton presented to the Congress an ingenious three-part plan for bringing the nation's finances into order and producing growth in the American economy.

First, the national government would pay off the national debt in full and would pay all the war debts of the individual states. Second, high tariffs (taxes) would be imposed on imported goods, which would help the development of American industries by increasing the price of imports. Third, the Congress would create a national bank for storing government funds and stabilizing the national currency.

These all were adopted, although none without controversy. The debt-payoff idea, for example, was not universally popular. Southern states, which generally had far less debt than the northern ones, saw it as unfair. But they dropped their objections when the northern states agreed to locate the permanent national capital (what would eventually be Washington, D.C.) in the Upper South on the Potomac River.

But a more serious debate, the first great debate about constitutional interpretation, was to erupt over the third idea, the creation of a national bank. Madison and his fellow Virginian Jefferson strongly opposed the idea, arguing that there was no basis in the Constitution for the creation of a such a bank and that such a bold move would violate both the letter and spirit of the Constitution as a charter of limited powers.

Hamilton disagreed. He believed that such an expansion of power was implicit in the Constitution and was stated fairly directly in Article I, section 8, which granted the Congress power to "make all Laws which shall be necessary and proper" for carrying out the functions of government. (This came to be known as the Constitution's "elastic clause.")

In the end, Washington sided with Hamilton, and the bank became a reality – and an instant success. Similarly successful was the bulk of Hamilton's entire bold economic program, which freed the nation from its heavy debt burdens in surprisingly short order and established a sound basis for a rapidly growing economy.

But the difference between Jefferson and Hamilton, and particularly the difference between "strict" and "loose" interpretations of the Constitution, would not go away so easily. For many years to come, in fact, the opposition between Jefferson and Hamilton would be at the center of national debates.

That opposition was so important because it went far beyond the two men's different views of the Constitution, beyond their intense rivalry and personal antagonism, and beyond their frequent disagreements within the Washington Cabinet. The two men symbolized two different ways of thinking about the kind of nation that the United States should become.

Hamilton was an urban man, a New Yorker intent upon building an expanding economy featuring extensive trade and manufacturing. He favored using a powerful and active central government to help create the conditions favoring such an economy. Jefferson, by contrast, was a gentleman farmer from Virginia who disliked cities and distrusted commerce and financial wizardry. He regarded government as a necessary evil, at best, to be kept as small as possible. He favored a mostly local form of government, and a society inhabited primarily by small, self-sufficient farmers.

Farming, Jefferson believed, was the way of life most favorable to the development of moral character in the citizenry. "Those who labor in the earth," he wrote, "are the chosen people of God." By contrast, he feared that if Hamilton were to get his way, the nation would develop a large class of wage laborers and other landless and propertyless men concentrated in the cities, highly dependent upon others for their well-being.

Nor were these matters the only source of the two men's opposition. When the French Revolution, which had begun in summer 1789, led to a major war between France and England, President Washington was presented with a sticky problem. Should the United

States give assistance to the French, who had, after all, been important allies in the American Revolution? Wasn't their desire to establish a republican form of government something that many Americans would gladly support? But what about the reports of bloody anarchy and mass executions in France, as the Revolution spun out of control? Jefferson, who sympathized with the revolutionary cause in France, and thought the British were corrupt and decadent by comparison, believed that American policy should show a preference for the French. Hamilton, who was known to be pro-British, had the opposite view, preferring the stability of British society to the chaos into which the Revolution in France had so quickly descended.

In the end, Washington followed neither advisor entirely. He insisted on a neutral course until the United States could grow stronger. He issued a proclamation to that effect on April 22, 1793, declaring the United States to be "friendly and impartial toward the belligerent powers" and cautioning American citizens against "aiding or abetting" either side. Jefferson was highly displeased with this action, which he believed favored the British, and resigned his position as secretary of state in furious opposition. But Washington understood that the needs of the nation, which was in no position to challenge the doings of a great power like England or France, made it necessary to steer clear of both sides.

Washington went to great lengths to stay on the path of neutrality, even risking unhappiness with his leadership coming from citizens who failed to understand how damaging a war could be at this time. There is no better example of this prudence on Washington's part than the controversial and deeply unpopular Jay Treaty (1794), negotiated with the British by Supreme Court chief justice (and Publius co-contributor) John Jay. The Jay Treaty pried the British out of their western frontier forts at last, eliminating a persistent and insulting thorn in the nation's side. But it did so at the price of letting the British off the hook for a great many legitimate claims against them.

Much of the American public reacted with outrage at this rather one-sided treaty, and Washington himself hesitated before signing it. In retrospect, though, it was an act of wise statesmanship to accept it. Nothing was more important to the future of the country than the calming of relations between the United States and Britain. But because of its political unpopularity, the Jay Treaty had the unsought side effect of drawing more Americans into the Jeffersonian camp and thus contributing to the nation's growing divisions.

Given the wide range of the Jefferson–Hamilton feud, it is no wonder that it turned out to be the source of the first system of opposing political parties in the history of the United States. In addition, it is no wonder that a national beginning with such huge hopes as the American one would attract many worries that the great national experiment was being betrayed.

We already saw these kinds of concerns come up during the debates over ratification. But the French Revolution sharpened them to a razor's edge. There was exaggeration on both sides. The Hamiltonians feared that Jefferson's followers were soft on mob rule and favored violent overthrow of established leaders. The Jeffersonians feared that Hamilton and his followers really wanted a king and that Hamilton's admiration for a vigorous central government and for Britain went hand in hand. Both sides feared that the other side did not have the country's best interests at heart.

Under such circumstances, the formation of political parties was almost unavoidable. Nevertheless, this development would be a bitter disappointment to a great many of the Framers. Nearly all of them, and particularly Washington himself, had hoped that political parties would never have a chance to arise under the new government, a position that seems somewhat unrealistic today.

In any event, the party lines that were steadily forming, pitting Hamilton's Federalist Party against Jefferson's Democratic Republicans, did not harden until after Washington stepped down from the presidency. This holding back was out of respect for the indispensable man himself, who continued to be a revered figure of national unity, like a great dam holding back flood waters, even as the fierce quarrel between the two opposing camps gathered strength.

By the end of a second term of office, however, Washington was ready to retire and at long last to return to Mount Vernon for good. He announced his decision to do so in a Farewell Address to the nation, delivered on September 17, 1796, the ninth anniversary of the adoption of the Constitution in Philadelphia, and then published in the nation's newspapers in fall 1796. It would be one of the most important speeches in American history.

The title was deceptive. The speech did much more than say goodbye. It was a deep reflection on the national condition, containing the "disinterested warnings of a parting friend." It was an effort on Washington's part to project his influence into the American future, summarizing his wisdom about questions of governing and voicing his worries about the new nation's current challenges. It became an instant classic and a point of reference in the centuries to come. Even today, the speech has much to tell us.

If his message could be summed up in a single word, that word would be *unity*. All around him, Washington saw evidence of growing divisions, which could only mean troubles to come. Washington began by making it clear how much he disliked "the baneful effects of the spirit of party," the bitterness that was pushing the nation into partisan politics. He expressed his concern about the related rise of sectional conflict, in which northerners and southerners and easterners and westerners all seemed to be placing their local interests above those of the country as a whole. They were forgetting all the ways in which their differences were necessary for the prospering of the whole.

The most lastingly influential part of the speech dealt with foreign affairs and America's proper attitude toward the rest of the world. In such matters, Washington advised being careful and aloof, always placing the interests of the American nation over other considerations. He firmly cautioned against citizens allowing "passionate attachments" to foreign nations and causes to outweigh their commitment to their own nation. In addition, he urged American citizens to be constantly on their guard against efforts by foreign countries to influence American politics to their own advantage.

The new American nation had a great advantage over all others because of its remoteness from Europe. It had the protective barrier of an entire ocean. That advantage should never be sacrificed, Washington cautioned. The needs of America should always come first. The controversies that had been shaking Europe since 1789 were "foreign to our concerns," and America should stay clear of them, avoiding all "permanent alliances," a formulation that well reflects the thinking behind his own policies. His warning that the United States should avoid foreign entanglements, especially permanent ones, remained a standard of American foreign policy for a century to come.

12 · THE RISE OF JEFFERSON

In the election of 1796, which would be the first contested election in American history, Washington's vice president, John Adams, defeated Thomas Jefferson, but only very narrowly. The closeness of his victory was a sign of growing strength of the Republican faction and discontent with the Federalists, who had been in power since 1789. So Adams began his administration with some disadvantages.

Perhaps the greatest disadvantage of all was that he would always be compared to his illustrious predecessor. If the general sentiment toward Washington was respect bordering on reverence, Adams produced something like the opposite. He lacked Washington's imposing stature and stately reserve. Instead, he was a short and stocky man, with a personality that could be vain, cranky, and easily roused to anger.

But Adams was also an extremely honest and public-spirited figure, one of the greatest of the patriots, having been a Revolutionary leader, a member of the Continental Congress, an effective diplomat who served the new nation with distinction in Europe, and a man of impressive intellectual sophistication and stubborn independence of mind. We know a great deal about his long and affectionate marriage to Abigail, a witty and capable woman who was fully his partner and equal. They kept up an extensive correspondence, a by-product of the months and years they were forced to spend apart due to his tireless service to his country. Through thick and thin, Abigail was his soulmate and most trusted advisor. In retrospect, this quirky and flawed but compulsively truthful man may be the most lovable of all the Founders.

As president, though, he was dealt a very tough hand. The spill-over from the ongoing French problem, which had been greatly worsened by public outrage over the Jay Treaty, threatened to engulf Adams's administration from the outset. French attacks on American shipping had long been a problem, and they were now increasing. When Adams attempted to negotiate with the French about the matter, his representatives were presented with a crude demand from three French diplomats (known only as X, Y, and Z) for a very large bribe as the precondition of their even being permitted to begin such negotiations. The Americans refused, and when Adams released their report to the public, revealing the French agents' outrageous and insulting demand, it caused an uproar and an abrupt reversal in the public's formerly affectionate view of France. "Millions for defense, but not one cent for tribute!" was the cry that went up throughout the country, and even some Republicans joined in the demand for war against the French as the only suitable answer.

Yet Adams resisted the feverish cries for a declaration of war, recognizing that the nation, which lacked a serious navy and had a grand total of thirty-five hundred men under arms, was not equipped for any such venture. It was a wise move, but one that did not endear him to the public. Making himself loved by the public was not one of John Adams's talents.

All this foreign turbulence also rocked the nation's internal politics. It led to a season of instability and genuine peril, in which the fragility of the nation's unity was made alarmingly clear. The Republicans had always favored friendly relations with France. But now they found themselves on the defensive about that. They had to choose between appearing to favor the revolutionary objectives of the French or supporting the position of their enemies, the Federalists.

Meanwhile, some of the more extreme elements among the Federalists saw in this situation a rare opportunity to corner and demolish their Republican opponents. They allowed themselves to believe, whether rationally or not, that the Republicans might well decide to side with the French in the event of war. If that were to happen, it would represent a clear threat to the nation, and so it should be prevented at all costs.

Claims of treason by Republicans and a flood of wild stories filled the public press – it was the 1790s version of "fake news" – and enraged the Federalists. Adding to their rage was the fact that Jefferson himself was a skilled and ruthless practitioner of tough electoral tactics. He would attack his enemies indirectly by planting rumors about them in the press or publish anonymous editorials against them – or hire writers to portray opponents like John Adams in a harshly negative light, as secret monarchists who longed to reign as kings. (The Federalists were not above doing the same thing, but they did not do it nearly as well.) In any event, the overheated atmosphere allowed the Federalists to push through Congress, and obtain Adams's signature for, legislation designed to suppress their critics and prevent foreign influence on American politics.

These were the infamous Alien and Sedition Acts of 1798, which authorized the president to expel "dangerous" foreigners at his pleasure and severely limited freedom of speech and the press. Adams did not originate the acts, but he did not hesitate to support them, and that proved to be a grave error on his part. The First Amendment's guarantees of freedom of speech and press were regarded by most Americans as fundamental to their way of life and therefore sacred. Yet those sacred guarantees were being set aside so that the party in power could go after its opposition more readily. It now became a crime to publish what someone else might judge to be "false, scandalous, and malicious" criticism of high government officials. Nor was this an idle threat – twenty-five Republican newspaper editors were prosecuted in the run-up to the election.

In angry response, Jefferson and Madison drafted the Kentucky and Virginia Resolutions, which denounced the Alien and Sedition Acts and declared that because the Constitution was a "compact" among already-existing states, the individual states had the right to reject or reverse acts of the national government that a state believed to be unconstitutional. In other words, they were saying that the individual states had the right to set aside federal law.

Such a proposition was just as reckless as the Alien and Sedition Acts, because if implemented, it would subvert the nation's entire constitutional structure. George Washington was appalled by them and warned Patrick Henry that, if pursued, such measures would "dissolve the union." The conflict had ratcheted up several notches and was moving into extremely dangerous territory.

Clearly both parties were veering out of control and supplying an object lesson in why George Washington loathed political parties. If the Alien and Sedition Acts had been excessive and dangerous in its suppression of free speech, so, too, were the doctrines being offered by Jefferson and Madison, which would have made the national government powerless. It seemed that in the heat of the moment, both sides of this controversy were losing their bearings and introducing ideas and practices that were opposed to the heart and soul of American constitutionalism.

As the election of 1800 approached, the Federalists painted their opponents as wild-eyed revolutionaries and atheists, who were bent upon plunging the nation into a bloody French-style social revolution. Meanwhile, the Republicans depicted the Federalists as monarchists and aristocrats, enemies of liberty and friends of the wealthy who were using government to reverse the effects of the American Revolution. To top it all off, Adams's statesmanlike but politically costly decision to seek peace with the French rather than go to war with them lost him essential political support from members of his own party.

It was an explosive situation in which anything could happen. All was in readiness for an extremely tough and close, election. Then, when it seemed things could not get worse, they did. In December 1799 came word of the death of George Washington, the great unifier whose presence had always pulled the nation together in the past. It seemed a very bad sign, to lose the indispensable man at this critical moment. Had something gone out of the nation's life and spirit along with him? Who or what in the current madhouse of conflict could possibly arise to take his place?

Such worries turned out to be unjustified, at least in the short term. In the end, Thomas Jefferson defeated Adams by a small but decisive margin, seventy-three electoral votes to Adams's sixty-five. The outcome was complicated by the fact that, due to a defect in the Constitution, which would soon be corrected by adoption of the Twelfth Amendment, Adams's vice presidential running mate Aaron Burr received the same number of electoral votes as Jefferson, and the matter had to be decided by a vote of the House of Representatives. But none of this complexity and drama can alter the fact that the outcome of the election was accepted by all parties as decisive and that it therefore represented a very important moment in the development of American government and society.

This was so for several reasons. Perhaps most importantly, the inauguration of Jefferson in 1801 was the first time that the orderly, peaceful, and legitimate transfer of power from one political party to another had taken place in the United States under the new Constitution. The importance of this achievement is hard to exaggerate. Almost every kind of political regime stumbles when it arrives at the threshold of a major transition. One of the best measures of stability in such a regime is precisely the ease, or difficulty, with which it handles the problem of succession, of replacing one leader with another.

Even under the best of circumstances, that can be difficult. Even the best ruler can be followed by a bad one who undoes the good his predecessor achieved. Even the best government can buckle under the pressures of war, social unrest, or economic depression. Even under the best of times, a transfer of power is risky, since it requires the initiation of something new, something that has not existed before.

And these were not the best of times. Given the intense circumstances under which the 1800 election took place, and the newness of the institutions that the Constitution had created, it could hardly have been a worse time to put the new Constitution to the test. How stable was a post-Washington America going to be? How sturdy could those institutions be – and how deeply had they been sunk into the hearts of the people? The fact that the electoral outcome might mean the defeat of a sitting president made the question even more challenging. What if he refused to leave office? What if there was armed resistance?

All these were legitimate questions. If someone had set out to design a situation in which Americans' respect for the law would be overwhelmed by their passions and their fears, he couldn't do much better than this. That the nation did get past this challenge, and did so not only peacefully but with surprising ease, was amazing – and the best sign imaginable for the future success of the American experiment.

In addition, the election of 1800 was an important transition because it marked a change of direction. The Republican victory would mean a movement in the direction of a somewhat greater degree of democracy, wider political participation, an acknowledged place for political parties in the American system, and a shift in the tone and direction of policy.

But one should not exaggerate the extent of these changes. Jefferson himself grandly referred, in an 1819 letter written long after his retirement from public life, to "the revolution of 1800," and many historians have followed him in employing that expression. But Jefferson was referring in those words not to new policies but merely to the peaceable transfer of power itself: the nation's success in producing change "not effected indeed by the sword ... but by the rational and peaceable instrument of reform, the suffrage [vote] of the people."

Indeed, Jefferson as president turned out to be a far less revolutionary leader than his enemies had feared or his friends had hoped. He signaled this would be the case in his first inaugural address, a speech nearly as masterly as Washington's Farewell, marked by its modesty ("the task is above me.... I approach it with anxious and awful presentiments"), its respect for the losing side ("the minority possess their equal rights, which equal law must protect"), and, above all, its desire to heal and unify the country ("Every difference of opinion is not a difference of principle.... We are all Republicans – we are all Federalists.")

He also signaled a generous tolerance of dissent and varied opinion: "If there be any among us who would wish to dissolve this Union or to change its republican form, let them stand undisturbed as monuments of the safety with which error of opinion may be tolerated where reason is left free to combat it." He concluded with a list of principles he would follow, none of which could be seen as controversial, and some of which echoed Washington's warnings against foreign entanglements very closely, and repeatedly invoked the same rights of Englishmen that had been respected since time immemorial, products of "the wisdom of our sages and the blood of our heroes," nearly all of them enshrined in the Bill of Rights.

It is hard to imagine a more winning and peacemaking speech for the occasion, and a more welcome relief for those who had feared for the future of the Union itself. Jefferson continued in the same calming and measured vein during his early days as president. While he would go on to make some policy changes, there were but few that could be called dramatic, let alone drastic. He made modest reductions in military expenditures, reduced taxes that the Federalists had imposed, and worked hard to pay down the national debt. But he accepted that Hamilton's financial program, which he had fought tooth and nail while in Washington's cabinet, was here to stay, and he made a point of indicating his support for it.

The "revolution of 1800" is better thought of, then, as a significant step forward in the unification and maturing of the new American nation. The Constitution itself was a great achievement, but from its ratification debates forward, it was in the process of being worked on, and worked out, in actual political practice. Jefferson was a man of ideas, but he was also a practical man. The party system that the Framers had not wanted had arisen anyway and turned out to serve the Constitution well, as a way not only to express and channel controversy but to organize it and contain it.

An important outward sign of this progress was the very place at which Jefferson took the presidential oath of office and delivered his address. It did not occur in New York or Philadelphia but, for the first time, in the brand-new capital city of Washington. The Washington of that time, of course, only faintly resembled the grand capital city of today, but even then, it possessed the bones of its later body, in the form of the grand urban design that French military engineer Pierre L'Enfant had been commissioned in 1791, by George Washington, to produce.

L'Enfant was a moody genius, and in the end he did not stay to finish his project. But thanks to the design he provided, Washington was destined to be unique among American cities. Most of those cities would be laid out to the extent possible as simple functional grids, a weave of north–south avenues and east–west streets. One might think, for example, of the central business districts of such cities as Chicago or New York as classic examples of urban grids. L'Enfant's Washington would include such a functional grid but also would place upon it a graceful network of wide diagonal avenues that interconnected through circles and squares, providing for an endless array of dramatic and unexpected vistas, as well as numerous park sites for the erection of statuary and monuments to remember and celebrate the unfolding national story.

Capitol Hill, site of the Congress, would be the center of the Federal City, and diagonal boulevards named after the states of the union would radiate out from it, from the President's House, and from a few other important nodes. Under L'Enfant's plan, the area west of the Capitol was to be a garden-lined public promenade, a "grand avenue" open to all comers, something that would have been unthinkable in L'Enfant's France but seemed to him perfectly appropriate to the more democratic spirit of the new United States. As indeed it was.

But the "grand avenue" L'Enfant planned was never built, and it was not until the twentieth century that the area, now known as the Mall, would be made into an open space, eventually to become home to the Smithsonian Institute and a distinguished collection of museums, as well as being a national stage and premier site for

public celebrations and political gatherings. As such, it would realize L'Enfant's essential intention, but in a way very different from
what he had in mind.

All that would still be many years into the future, though. At the
time of Jefferson's inauguration, Washington, D.C., was little more
than a village. It was not uncommon to find farm animals grazing
on the grassy land, content as if they were in the countryside. At
this moment in the city's history, a mere ten years into its construction, Washington, D.C., was still a very rough work in progress, like
the nation itself. But like the nation, the city had begun life with a
brilliant founding plan, and like the nation, it would now take
shape according to that plan.

13 · THE JEFFERSON PRESIDENCY

THE CONTRAST BETWEEN Thomas Jefferson's presidency and those before it was partly a matter of style. Washington and Adams both sought to surround the presidency with an aura of grandeur and high dignity. The image-conscious Washington insisted on traveling in a grand carriage drawn by a team of white horses. Such impressive self-presentation was not for the sake of feeding Washington's ego. Instead, he meant it to serve an important public purpose, that of increasing citizens' respect for the office of the presidency.

Such splendor troubled those of a more republican sensibility, who feared that the ideas and practices of kings might infect the new office of the presidency. For that reason Jefferson chose not to follow his predecessors' example. On the day of his inauguration, he decided to walk rather than ride to and from the Capitol, and he went on to establish a tone of low-key, simple republican informality in his dress, his manners, and his way of entertaining visitors at the brand-new presidential residence known as the White House.

But the Jefferson administration had its own kind of glamour. Jefferson was not an especially gifted public speaker, but he made up for it with a dazzling intellect and personal charm, all which he put to effective use in intimate dinner parties at the White House with carefully chosen members of Congress, Federalist and Republican alike. On these occasions, he would serve his guests the superb food produced by his French chef and give them excellent wines, all the while engaging in brilliant conversation, getting to know them better than they realized, and subtly working his influence on them.

Don't be deceived, though. There was an iron fist beneath his velvet glove. Jefferson was a far more partisan figure than his predecessors. He embraced the role of party leader and, unlike Washington and Adams, appointed only men of his own party to the top cabinet positions. Over the two terms of his presidency, he had great success in establishing Republican dominance and putting the Federalist party out of business.

Even so, one area of the national government escaped his control and remained in the hands of the Federalists: the judiciary.

This was extremely frustrating to Jefferson. Like many of his Anti-Federalist and Republican allies, he had a dislike for judges and for the use of judicial power and authority. This wasn't surprising. The judiciary was, after all, the least democratic branch of government, deliberately shielded from the influence of politics and public opinion. Instead, it drew its authority from the objectivity and permanence of the laws and from precedents that living people had little or no role in making.

And that offended Jefferson's democratic sensibilities. "No society," he wrote to Madison in 1789, "can make a perpetual constitution, or even a perpetual law. The earth belongs always to the living generation." In addition, Jefferson distrusted the tendency of judges to extend their powers – or, in his colorful phrase, "to throw an anchor ahead, and grapple further hold for future advances of power" – all of it in ways designed to get around the will of the people as expressed in their democratic institutions.

These complaints were not just about matters of philosophy. Once Jefferson became president, they became practical and immediate. He was infuriated that Adams had, in the last days of his presidency, appointed the Virginia Federalist John Marshall, a distant cousin to Jefferson whom he disliked, as chief justice of the Supreme Court. Then Adams had gone on, by means of the hastily passed Judiciary Act of 1801, to create six new federal circuit courts and staff them entirely with Federalists, from the judges down to the clerks. Thanks to these rather crafty moves, the judiciary would remain a Federalist stronghold for years to come, with Marshall serving as a very commanding chief justice for an astounding thirty-four years, until 1835.

Much of the Court's enduring influence owed to the leadership of Marshall. Yet he was an unlikely candidate for that role. He was not widely read in the law and had no previous judicial experience. But he made up for those disadvantages with his strong sense of the Court's proper place in the constitutional order and his ability to move events and cases toward achieving that goal. It was clear to a great many Americans after their experiences with the Alien and Sedition Acts that there needed to be some check on the executive and legislative branches, to serve as insurance against another such time of inflamed and unconstitutional actions.

It seems certain that the Framers had wanted for the Supreme Court to play such a role, but they failed to spell out exactly how the check would operate. Marshall succeeded in establishing just such a check, the Court's right of *judicial review*, through the 1803 case of *Marbury v. Madison*, the first important case to come before his Court, and a truly impressive example of Marshall's skillfulness in pursuing his goals.

It was a crafty decision, just the kind of judicial move that made Jefferson's blood boil. The roots of the case involved Adams's "midnight" appointments to the circuit courts that had so angered Jefferson. When Jefferson discovered that several of the documents appointing justices of the peace in the District of Columbia had accidentally not been mailed out, even though they had been signed by Adams, Jefferson decided to hold on to them, thus effectively stopping delivery of the appointments themselves. In response, one of the appointees, William Marbury, sued for a court order (called a *writ of mandamus*) that would force Madison, who served as Jefferson's secretary of state, to deliver Marbury's commission.

This situation presented Marshall with a sticky problem. If he refused to issue the order, it would avoid a collision with the new administration, but it would appear that he was giving in to Jefferson, a perception that would set a bad precedent. Not only that, but it would damage the prestige and independence of the Court and undermine the separation of powers – not to mention depriving the judiciary of another Federalist judge! And besides, Marbury had a rather strong claim to the position, which was being denied him on a technicality.

But if Marshall agreed to issue the order to grant Marbury his commission, it was possible that Madison would ignore him, and the mood of the country, still sour toward the Federalists, would likely back Madison up. Such a turn of events would be a disaster for the Court, because it would amount to an advertisement of the Court's lack of power. That, too, would undermine the separation of powers. What, then, was he to do?

The strategy he arrived at was ingenious. First, he argued that yes, Marbury had a right to his commission, under his reading of the Judiciary Act of 1789, which had set up the federal court system in the first place. But the clause that Marbury invoked was, Marshall argued, unconstitutional. Congress could not legally grant the Supreme Court the power to issue writs of mandamus. This in turn meant that the law Marbury was invoking was not valid and could not be used to further his claims. Marbury therefore would not be able to receive his commission.

Do you follow that? The brilliance of this tactic might not be immediately apparent. But it is important to keep in mind that the work of courts, and especially courts of appeal, is built around the authority of legal *precedents*. And like a chess master who sacrifices a valuable piece in order to secure a victory, Marshall sacrificed Marbury's commission to take possession of something much larger. He refrained from pursuing a small and unimportant Federalist gain (Marbury as a single Federalist judge) in exchange for a precedent that could be used again and again, because it established the independent power of the Supreme Court to rule an act of Congress unconstitutional.

He gave Jefferson the decision Jefferson wanted, but did it by means of reasoning that Jefferson did not want at all. But there was nothing that Jefferson could do about it, since the immediate result of the decision was completely in line with his wishes. It was the *reasoning*, not the result, that would prove to be more important in the end.

Talk about throwing an anchor ahead, and grappling toward future advances of power! And this gain was made all the more annoying to Jefferson because of the Federalist domination of the courts. Jefferson was not through fighting yet and went on to resist judicial Federalism by pressing for the removal of judges whom he considered particularly bad and partisan. But that campaign failed miserably. Jefferson badly overreached in trying to remove Samuel Chase, a Revolutionary-era patriot and associate justice of the Supreme Court.

With only one exception, the Federalist judges remained in place. Marshall was left largely unchallenged and, through a series of landmark decisions passed down during his many years in office, was able to strengthen the hand of the Court and of the central government – notwithstanding the dominance of Jefferson's party and its banishment of the Federalists from executive and legislative power. He would manage this by proceeding in a steady, methodical, case-by-case way, along the path that he had already pioneered with *Marbury v. Madison*.

So even despite Jefferson's popularity during most of his presidency, he had to accept a measure of compromise with the opposition, just as he had accepted most of the Hamiltonian economic program to achieve national peace. Jefferson came into office with his own vision of the American future and well-developed ideas and firm convictions about the right ordering of political society. But like every president in the nation's history, he had to adjust his ideas to the realities of practical politics in a complex and changing world.

Nor was this acceptance of the Federalist legacy the only way that Jefferson had to depart sharply from his principles.

Perhaps the single greatest achievement of his presidency was the American acquisition of the Louisiana Territory, the lands to the west of the then existing United States, an act that more than doubled the size of the country and at the same time removed a foreign presence from the western border of the nation. It was the act that opened the way for the United States to go from being a coastal nation to a sprawling continental one.

But it was also an act that involved Jefferson in a violation of the Constitution – and certainly a violation of Jefferson's own understanding of the Constitution and of the principles of constitutional interpretation, as he had insisted upon them in his fierce battles with Hamilton during the Washington administration.

The lands in question had belonged to the French, and for a time, it appeared that Napoleon Bonaparte, the rising French military and political leader, was interested in reviving the French empire in the New World. This rightly alarmed Jefferson. He sent his political ally James Monroe, then governor of Virginia, to join ambassador Robert R. Livingston in France. They had permission from Jefferson to spend up to $10 million to purchase the city of New Orleans, which controlled commerce on the Mississippi and thus represented a potential danger to American trade. Whoever controlled New Orleans could control all of the trade that came through it, which meant controlling the economic life of central North America.

When Monroe joined Livingston in Paris, they discovered that the French had experienced a change of heart about reviving their North American empire. Much to their surprise, the French offered to sell *all* the Louisiana Territory, a huge swath of land between the Mississippi River and the Rocky Mountains, extending north from the Gulf of Mexico to present-day Montana and west as far as Colorado and Wyoming, for a mere $15 million, or 60 million francs. Livingston and Monroe did not hesitate. Even though it meant exceeding their instructions, they said yes to the offer and signed a treaty.

Clearly they were right to do so; it was the deal of the century, if not the millennium. But it left Jefferson with a dilemma. He and nearly all Americans clearly saw the benefit of the Louisiana Purchase to the nation's future. For Jefferson, who wanted the United States to stay a primarily agricultural country for as long as possible, the Purchase was a godsend, making available vast tracts of land that could allow the nation's future development to take an agricultural direction – and to do so at a small cost. He could not say no.

But there was a problem. There was nothing in the Constitution authorizing a president to add new territory to the United States by the purchase of land. Jefferson was now caught between his high principles and the practical demands of governing. It would have been unwise to pass up this offer. But how could it be justified within Jefferson's strict-constructionist reading of the Constitution?

He dithered for a while and tried to come up with a constitutional amendment, either before or after the Senate ratified the treaty, but finally concluded that the best path ahead would be to ignore the "metaphysical subtleties" of the issue; "the less we say about constitutional difficulties the better." Congress ratified the treaty, and that was that. Jefferson would cruise to reelection in 1804, and his popularity would soar as never before.

It made for a very complex picture. Just as Jefferson accepted the Hamiltonian economic program rather than reverse it, so, too, did he reinforce the Hamiltonian interpretation of the Constitution, rather than reversing it, by means of the single greatest use of executive power in the country's history to that point. And at the same time, he boosted his own power, and the power of his party, for a generation to come. The fortunes of the Federalist Party sank further and further – even though Jefferson's actions would seem to have supported Federalist principles far more than they did his!

It would not be the last time that a president would find it necessary to support some of the very things he had opposed before taking office – not from lack of principle, but out of political necessity. It only added to the complexity of it all that a bitter group of defeated Federalists in New England, known as the Essex Junto (because so many of them were from Essex County, Massachusetts), began hatching schemes to secede from the Union and tried,

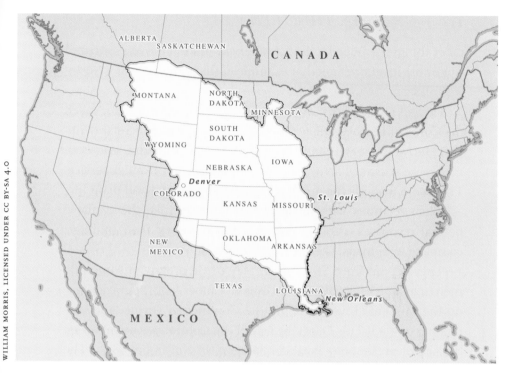

The Louisiana Purchase, superimposed upon the boundaries of the present-day states. At the time of the acquisition of Louisiana, most of the area to the south and west was owned by Spain.

unsuccessfully, to get Hamilton to join them. Federalists as secessionists and Republicans as nationalists! The world did seem to be turning upside down again.

But with the acquisition of the vast Louisiana Territory, it was as if a page of history was being turned and a new chapter begun, with a whole rich field of activity in the American interior being opened up for the American people. Jefferson, whose lively intellectual interests included a passion for scientific knowledge and research, could hardly wait to find out what mysteries and wonders awaited the nation in these new uncharted territories. In fact, he had already been planning a coast-to-coast scientific expedition even before the chance to acquire all of Louisiana fell in his lap. Among other things, he hoped to find a waterway linking the Missouri and Columbia Rivers, yet another example of that old dream of a Northwest Passage, refusing to die.

He had already been organizing an exploratory mission, called the Corps of Discovery Expedition, led by his private secretary Captain Meriwether Lewis and Second Lieutenant William Clark. Both men were seasoned army officers with a record of frontier service. They were to study the area's geography and animal and plant life, establish relations with the native peoples, and list the available natural resources – and to deliver a full report of their findings, complete with maps, sketches, and journals.

They set out from St. Louis in May 1804, a party of some fifty men in a large keelboat and two dugout canoes, and, after traveling up the Missouri River, crossing the Continental Divide, and proceeding to the Pacific Ocean by way of the Columbia River, reached the site of present-day Portland, Oregon, in November 1805. The expedition was aided by a young Lemhi Shoshone woman named Sacagawea, who accompanied the expedition over the many miles from the Dakota region to the Pacific Ocean, helping to establish peaceful contacts with the Native peoples along the way. After accumulating an amazing record of adventures, and an even more astonishing treasury of information and artifacts relating to the lands through which they had passed, Lewis and Clark finally returned to St. Louis in September 1806, receiving universal praise.

The national celebration over the triumphant return of Lewis and Clark showed that the exploration and settlement of the vast American West was becoming an important focus of the nation's energies. But there were still nagging questions of foreign relations to be resolved. Most of these problems revolved around the American effort to protect its trade and avoid having to take sides in wars taking place in the larger world. These problems complicated the last years of Jefferson's time as president.

First, Jefferson sought to reverse his predecessors' practice of paying bribes to pirates from the Barbary States of North Africa as a way of buying protection for American shipping in the Mediterra-

New England theologian and minister Jonathan Edwards (1703–58), one of the greatest preachers of the Great Awakening.

Benjamin Franklin (1705–90), the man who represented the Enlightenment in America, and one of the greatest of the Founders, painted during Franklin's time in France.

A political cartoon from 1754 that became a very popular image and was used to encourage the idea of unifying the British colonies of North America into one nation.

Paul Revere's engraving called The Bloody Massacre in King-Street, *a powerful expression of anti-British feelings.*

George Washington (1732–99), the indispensable man, a victorious general and wise political leader who commanded the respect of nearly all who knew him.

Thomas Jefferson (1743–1826) in the triumphant year of 1800, when he was elected president. He was author of the Declaration of Independence and a man of lofty ideals but also a bundle of contradictions who feared that conflict over slavery might eventually tear the nation apart.

The master pamphleteer Thomas Paine (1737–1809), whose 1776 pamphlet called Common Sense *helped to unite the colonists behind the goal of American independence.*

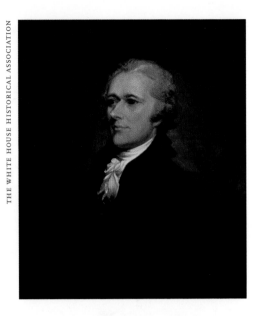

James Madison (1751–1836), the architect of the Constitution. He was a very small man, but he cast a large shadow over American history.

Alexander Hamilton (1775?–1804), the economic wizard of the nation's early history and archenemy of Thomas Jefferson.

John Adams (1735–1826), second president of the United States, in his official presidential portrait.

Abigail Adams (1744–1818), John Adams's wife, advisor, and frequent correspondent, the other half of one of the great marriages of early American history.

The L'Enfant Plan for Washington, D.C., which created the underlying structure of what became one of the most beautiful cities in the world.

Lewis and Clark on the Lower Columbia, *by Charles Marion Russell (1864–1926), one of the master artists of the American West. The painting depicts the red-haired William Clark, who stands in his canoe with a flintlock rifle cradled in his arms, while his party's Shoshone guide, Sacagawea, communicates by sign language with a group of Columbia River Indians.*

Andrew Jackson (1767–1845). Notice the contrast between his image and that of Thomas Jefferson. Where Jefferson is aristocratic and composed, Jackson is the man of action, with windswept hair and chiseled features, a face hardened by war.

Abolitionist Frederick Douglass (1818–95). Born a slave, he escaped that condition, and transformed himself into one of the greatest orators of his time, a living refutation of the very idea of racial inequality.

Harriet Beecher Stowe (1811–96), author of the great novel Uncle Tom's Cabin (1852).

Ralph Waldo Emerson (1803–82), prophet of a new American culture and author of America's "intellectual Declaration of Independence."

Abraham Lincoln (1809–65) campaigning for the presidency in New York City, February 27, 1860.

Notice the weariness in President Abraham Lincoln's face in this picture, taken on February 5, 1865, less than five years after the above photograph in New York City. The war had taken an enormous toll on him.

Harriet Tubman (1822?–1913), abolitionist and legendary "conductor" in the Underground Railroad. A deeply committed Christian, she saw the plight of enslaved Americans escaping to freedom reflected in the biblical story of the Exodus, when the people of Israel came out of slavery in Egypt into the land God had promised them.

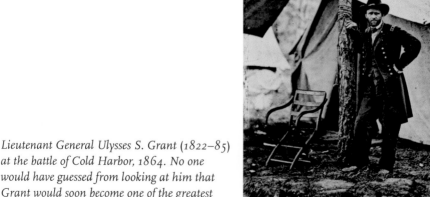

Lieutenant General Ulysses S. Grant (1822–85) at the battle of Cold Harbor, 1864. No one would have guessed from looking at him that Grant would soon become one of the greatest generals of history.

*he ruins of Richmond, Virginia,
fter its surrender in April 1865.*

The Grand Review of the Union Army, as depicted in Harper's Weekly *(1865). It was a parade
unlike any other that had ever been held in American history, marking the conclusion of the
Civil War.*

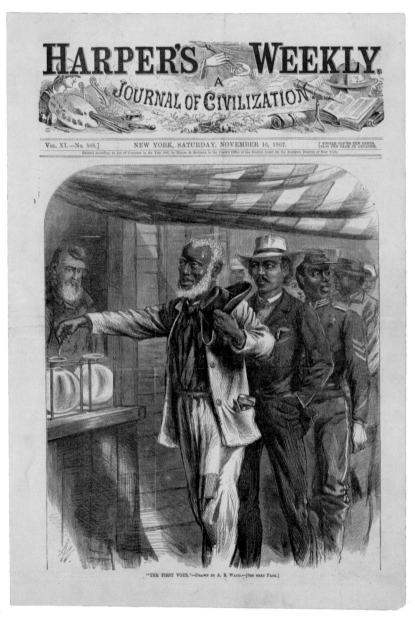

"The First Vote," drawn for Harper's Weekly, November 16, 1867, depicting a group of African Americans exercising their constitutional right to vote for the first time. Notice their varied clothing, including the man wearing the uniform of the Union Army, a reminder of the participation of freedmen in the war effort after the Emancipation Proclamation.

nean. By sending a small fleet of the U.S. Navy to the region, he gained a measure of respect and protection for American trade in the area. Score one victory for Jefferson.

Much more difficult were the problems with the British. The United States still found itself caught in the middle of the struggle between the British and the French, at a time when British control of the seas and French control of the landmass of Continental Europe were near complete. Each was trying to use economic warfare to cripple or disable the other. The American doctrine of neutral rights, permitting the United States to trade with all countries equally, was not going to be workable under the circumstances. The British especially rejected American neutral claims, with the practice of seizing American sailors, whom they claimed to be British citizens, and "impressing" them into service in the British navy.

Like Washington and Adams before him, Jefferson did not want war, and in fact his reductions in military spending had made the weak American military even weaker. As an alternative, he persuaded the Congress to pass the Embargo Act in 1807, which prohibited American merchant ships from sailing into foreign ports. He hoped that British dependence on American goods and shipping would force their hand and lead to a peaceful settlement of the issues.

But unfortunately, the Embargo failed. It caused far more hardship at home than it did to Britain, which was easily able to find substitutes for the lost American trade. It caused a near-depression in the New England states, which revived the Essex Junto by rallying public opposition to a much-hated law. Finally, as one of Jefferson's last acts as president, he called for the repeal of the Embargo.

Jefferson could have run for election a third time; there was no constitutional barrier to it. But he believed in following Washington's example of retiring from office after two terms. He thought it was a practice that was fitting for a genuine republican form of government, in which the people rule and the title of "citizen" is the highest rank available. Even if he had not believed that, though, he would have been likely to retire. Four years after winning reelection by a lopsided margin, his fortunes had turned for the worse.

He was leaving office a tired and discouraged man, defeated by seemingly unsolvable problems, and overwhelmed with headaches, rheumatism, and other physical ailments.

He came to refer to his presidential experience as "splendid misery" and even seemed to wonder for a time whether he had been miscast for his role in politics. He wondered whether he was made for a quieter existence. As he wrote to a French economist friend, just before the end of his second term, "Never did a prisoner, released from his chains, feel such relief as I shall on shaking off the shackles of power. Nature intended me for the tranquil pursuits of science, by rendering them my supreme delight. But the enormities of the times in which I have lived, have forced me to … commit myself on the boisterous ocean of political passions. I thank God for the opportunity of retiring from them."

But the sixty-five-year-old Jefferson was not done yet, and his energies were soon restored by leaving politics behind and returning to his beloved home, Monticello, outside Charlottesville. Not only he did he busy himself with scientific work, one of his life's pure joys, but he would go on to establish the University of Virginia, an important step toward the fulfillment of his grand democratic dream of a free public education for all comers, irrespective of their social class or economic level.

If there was a central feature of Jefferson's idea of democracy, it was his belief in education as the great equalizer, the force that could potentially raise any man to the level of any other – and education as the essential factor in forming citizens who would be capable of self-rule. "The qualifications for self government in society," he wrote to Edward Everett in 1824, "are not innate. They are the result of habit and long training." Or, as he had said several years before, in rather more gloomy tones, "If a nation expects to be ignorant and free, in a state of civilization, it expects what never was and never will be."

Jefferson said many things of enduring importance, but none more important than this. It is a warning we would do well to heed today.

14 · AN ERA OF MIXED FEELINGS

With the election of 1808 and Jefferson's retirement, the problem of the British was now passed to his successor, James Madison. His two terms as president would be dominated by that problem and would, despite all efforts to the contrary, result in war. And as had so often been the case before, the sources of conflict were the violation of America's neutral rights at sea, which now involved the French as well as the British, and also the ongoing conflicts with the British over the western American frontier.

This time around, however, things were different. For one thing, the small and soft-spoken Madison was no match for the forces that were gathering on all sides and driving the movement toward war. Madison found himself overwhelmed. He was unable to restrain the British, unable to arrive at an workable trade policy with the warring countries, and unable to control the growing divisions at home.

Settlers on the frontier continued to press for expansion, which provoked resentment and violence from the Indian tribes that were losing more and more of their land. In response, the Shawnee warrior leader Tecumseh attempted to unite all the tribes east of the Mississippi into an Indian confederacy. This Indian hostility was blamed on British influence, operating especially through the Canadian province of Ontario. A group of young and intensely nationalistic Republican congressmen, dubbed the "War Hawks," would be satisfied with nothing less than an invasion of Canada! Madison was in an impossible spot.

Thus, despite the continued low level of American military preparedness, Madison yielded to the accumulating pressure and reluctantly asked for a declaration of war on June 1, 1812. Unknown to him, the British had already decided at the same time to end their interference with American shipping. But thanks to the difficulties of communication across an ocean, their decision was not known in America until it was too late. War had been declared, and war took on a momentum of its own.

About the war itself, which came to be known as the War of 1812, the best that can be said is that the United States was lucky to get out of it in one piece. Had the British not been occupied with fighting against Napoleon in Europe, the war would almost certainly have had a terrible effect upon the Americans. Indeed, after Napoleon's defeat in 1814, the British began to win a string of victories against the Americans, including the capture and burning of Washington, D.C., that could easily have led to the war being a complete humiliation for the United States. In addition, the war was deeply unpopular in the Federalist northern states, where it was called "Mr. Madison's War," and opposition to it nearly led a convention of New England states meeting in Hartford, Connecticut in December 1814 to consider withdrawing from the Union.

Fortunately, by then, there had been a few significant American triumphs, notably the defense of Fort McHenry in Baltimore against British attack, where the proud survival of the American flag inspired a lawyer named Francis Scott Key to write the lyrics to what would become "The Star-Spangled Banner," the eventual national anthem. More importantly, a war-weary Britain was ready to call it quits and find a settlement that would save face for all. The resulting Treaty of Ghent in December 1814 simply restored things to the way they were at the war's start. It was to be as if nothing had happened. Of course, with the war against Napoleon out of the picture, the very reason for the war in the first place, as a struggle over neutral rights at sea, had largely disappeared.

But there was one unexpected bright spot for the Americans, again a result of the slow speed of transatlantic communications.

A British force had been sent to New Orleans to capture the city and cut off the West from the rest of the country. It was met by General Andrew Jackson and his unusual force of frontier militiamen, pirates, free blacks, and French Creoles. The British regulars regarded the Americans with contempt and made a frontal assault on them on January 8, 1815. But Jackson's forces, which included some highly skilled marksmen, turned out to be more than equal to the challenge. They managed to create well-fortified positions from which they were able to rain down deadly artillery and gunfire upon the British and defeat them resoundingly. It was a smashing, thoroughly impressive American victory, perhaps the most impressive in the nation's history to date. For many Americans, the glory of it more than made up for all the humiliations that had come before.

Even so, the great victory at New Orleans came after the peace treaty had been signed at Ghent. That meant it didn't influence the treaty deliberations. But that did not mean that it was of no importance – far from it. For one thing, the resounding victory ensured that the treaty would be ratified quickly by both governments; there would be no dilly-dallying or revisiting of the issues.

But more importantly, this notable win allowed the United States to come out of an ill-considered, badly waged, and carelessly misconceived war with its head held high, and with something to be proud of. It had demonstrated its military strength and had acquired a greatly heightened sense of national pride – not to mention a new national hero.

There was yet another consequence. It is worth noting that the Republicans and Federalists once again had switched roles, the former playing the role of the vigorous nationalists, the latter taking the role of those advocating for states' rights and strict construction of the Constitution. Such a switch had happened before, at the end of Jefferson's administration.

This time around, however, the Federalists' position assumed a darker aspect than before. They would become associated in the public mind with the wartime disloyalty of the Hartford Convention, a disgrace from which the once-great party would never recover. Jackson's great triumph at New Orleans was the icing on that cake, and the many songs, speeches, celebrations, and commemorations of that victory often contained a criticism, open or implied, of the Federalists.

It soon became clear that the Federalist Party would be the greatest casualty of the War of 1812. Its days as a national party were numbered. It managed to field a presidential candidate in 1816, but that would be its last such effort. The "Virginia Dynasty" that had dominated the presidency since 1789, interrupted only by John Adams's single term, would continue with little or no opposition. James Monroe ran unopposed in 1820, and by 1824, the Federalist Party had collapsed altogether. With its collapse came also an end to the first party system of the United States and a period of complete Republican dominance.

Thus the War of 1812, for all of its military inconclusiveness, had major effects in other respects. With the war's end, the nation was soon on the road to being largely free of its entanglements in European affairs. It would be able to concentrate – at last! – on the pursuit of its own internal ambitions without major distractions, following the path laid out in Washington's Farewell Address.

There were a few remaining issues to tidy up. First, a series of agreements with the British resolved some nagging issues relating to the Great Lakes, fishing rights in Canadian waters, and boundary questions in the Pacific Northwest. Then, through a combination of diplomatic skill and aggressive military action by General Andrew Jackson, the United States was able to acquire all of Florida from Spain in 1821. There could be no doubt; it had taken nearly a half-century, but the United States was at last moving into a position where it could exert control over its part of the world.

These changed circumstances would be expressed as U.S. policy two years later in what came to be known as the Monroe Doctrine. The gist of the Doctrine was fairly simple: the western hemisphere was henceforth to be considered off limits to further European colonization, and any effort to the contrary, including European meddling or troublemaking in the newly independent former Spanish and Portuguese colonies of Latin America, would be regarded as "the manifestation of an unfriendly disposition toward the United States" and "dangerous to our peace and safety."

The Monroe Doctrine was taking the position that, while the western hemisphere had been a battleground of the European powers for centuries, it was now time for that to come to an end. The New World had risen to a status equal to, but independent of, the Old World. The statement also included a promise not to interfere in the affairs of any of the European powers. The United States would stay clear of Europe, just as it expected Europe to stay out of American affairs.

The Monroe Doctrine was in one sense merely an expression of the American doctrine of neutrality toward the European powers, looking back to Washington's Farewell Address. But it was politically daring, even a bit risky. It had no standing in international law, so other nations were not required to respect it. And the United States lacked the Navy to enforce it on its own, had it been challenged to do so.

But timing is everything in history, and the Doctrine was put forward at a moment when the European powers had no desire to challenge it. So the principles it asserted were allowed to stand. It would go on to become a cornerstone of American foreign policy, its influence lasting well into the twentieth century. It defined a distinctively American way of understanding the relationship between the Old World and the New World, by asserting that the former's political systems were "essentially different" from that of the latter.

Most of all, it expressed a sense of freedom that the country would finally be able to pursue its own destiny. It could flex its own muscles and seek its own destiny. A strong sense of nationalism flowed into every sphere of American life, from the surging economy to the rising sense of America as a distinct, if not yet fully realized, culture.

The economy deserves our attention here, because it was increasingly becoming a *national* economy. In the years immediately after the War of 1812, Representative Henry Clay of Kentucky proposed what became known as the American System, as an instrument for fostering economic growth. Although Clay was a member of Jefferson's Republican Party, his ideas clearly echoed Hamilton's. He called for high tariffs to protect American industries, the restoration of the National Bank (whose charter had been allowed to lapse in 1811), and internal improvements, which meant what we today might call "infrastructure": roads, canals, and other improvements designed to create an ever-more efficient system of national transportation.

The idea of federal support of internal improvements, while extremely popular in the West, was controversial in the older eastern states and did not enjoy much success until the twentieth century. In 1817, President Madison vetoed a Congressional bill that would have established a fund for internal improvements, finding the idea unconstitutional. Only the Old National Road, which ran from Cumberland, Maryland, to Wheeling, in what was then western Virginia, and eventually west to Vandalia, Illinois, was constructed by the U.S. government. (Today that same road is U.S. Route 40 and has been designated the Historic National Road.)

So, the building of turnpikes and other internal improvements would be the responsibility of states and private businessmen for the foreseeable future. That did not slow things down much, because there were so many such projects being built, with networks of privately funded toll roads arising to connect the nation's major cities. There was also a boom in the construction of inland waterways, such as the 363-mile-long Erie Canal in upstate New York. This remarkable engineering feat was strongly supported by New York governor De Witt Clinton, who predicted that such a canal would make New York City "the granary of the world, the emporium of commerce, the seat of manufactures, the focus of great moneyed operations.... The whole of Manhattan, covered with habitations and replenished with a dense population, will constitute one vast city."

Rarely has a politician's prophecy been grander – and never more on target. The Erie Canal connected the American interior with its coasts, the economies of western farms with those of eastern port cities. It led to a period of intense economic growth and canal building all over the country. The cities of Buffalo, Rochester, Syracuse, and other towns along the Erie Canal flourished, and exactly as Clinton predicted, New York City, the end point for most of the canal's traffic, soon became the nation's greatest commercial center.

Nor was that all. The first railroad lines were built in the 1820s and, by the 1830s, were beginning to give the canals a run for their money, transforming western towns like Chicago into major centers of commerce and population. That was a trend that would only continue and grow as the century rolled on. And coming at the same time as these improvements in transportation, a cluster of inventions helped to spur economic growth. Some of these were products of the nation's first years, whose potential was finally being realized in the more dynamic postwar environment.

A few examples: there was immigrant Samuel Slater's development of the factory system, which dramatically changed textile manufacturing in New England; Eli Whitney's development of the cotton gin, which made possible the development of cotton as a highly profitable crop that could be exported to other countries; John Fitch's and Robert Fulton's pioneering development of steamboat technologies and services; and Oliver Evans's development of machines that could vastly improve the milling of flour.

There were also important changes in the law that spurred economic growth. It was very expensive to build and operate the new factories, as well as the new roads, canals, and railroads that served them. Not even the richest families could afford the vast sums of money involved. But new state laws allowed for the creation of *corporations*, which could raise the necessary funds by allowing investors to purchase *shares* of the business, in exchange for a share of the company's profits.

The total effect of all these developments, accompanied as they were by the country's steady population growth and the physical expansion of the country, led to something even greater than the purely economic gains, as great as those were. It was causing a more subtle, more profound change in the nation's idea of itself.

Jefferson had hoped for an America of independent farmers who would live in sturdy, dignified, and self-reliant separateness from one another. That independence hadn't disappeared. But the America coming into being was connected, knit together, bit by bit, piece by piece, a process that advanced with every road that was constructed, every canal that was dug, every new city that established itself, and every product that found its way into a growing national marketplace. America was becoming as much a land of growing economic connectedness as it was one of sturdy self-reliance.

These things all made possible the development of a national spirit. But as the nation at long last turned its gaze inward, and westward, it soon saw, gazing back at it, the troubling problem it had failed to resolve at Philadelphia in 1787. The expansion of the nation could not help but raise the problem anew by forcing a decision about whether slavery would be permitted in the nation's newly created states. Each decision would entail, in some measure, revisiting the original decision, an act that became steadily more difficult for some, and more inescapable for others.

But at least there had been an effort, ever since Vermont joined the union as a free state and Kentucky as a slave state, to keep the number of northern free states and southern slave states in balance. By 1818, there were eleven of each category, so that state membership in the Senate would be equal, and each section would have the power to check the other. This was not a solution to the

The United States circa 1827 by New York mapmaker Amos Lay.

problem; it was at best a way of holding the problem at bay and keeping the growth of slavery within bounds.

Then, in 1819, the territory of Missouri applied to be admitted as a state, the first of the Louisiana Purchase territories to do so, and the problem was immediately elevated to crisis level. Slavery was already well established in the Missouri Territory, and there was no doubt that Missouri would seek to be admitted as a slave state. But doing so would disturb the balance of states. There were fiery debates in the Congress over the merits of Missouri's case and whether restrictions on slavery could be imposed as a condition of its admission to the Union.

The immediate problem was avoided by a compromise. The

state of Maine, carved out of the northern part of Massachusetts, would be admitted as a free state, and slavery would be excluded from the rest of the Louisiana Territory north of the 36°30′ line, which was Missouri's southern boundary extended westward. Thus the balance would be maintained, and this sudden flashpoint would die down, for the time being, with the 36°30′ line providing a rule by which the rest of the Louisiana Territory could be organized on the question.

But a problem postponed is not a problem solved, and wise observers knew it. Nor was it possible to have the easy confidence of so many of the Framers in Philadelphia, such as Sherman and Ellsworth, that slavery was an institution already on the path to extinction. Not anymore.

Thomas Jefferson, writing to his friend John Holmes from his peaceful Monticello retirement, confessed that "this momentous question, like a fire bell in the night, awakened and filled me with terror. I considered it at once as the knell of the Union. It is hushed indeed for the moment. But this is a reprieve only, not a final sentence." He never spoke more darkly, or more prophetically. A *knell* is the slow, solemn ringing of a bell for a death or a funeral. And he went on to express his sense of the difficulty of moving past the issue with a haunting image: "We have the wolf by the ear, and we can neither hold him, nor safely let him go."

15 · ENTER ANDREW JACKSON

Over the course of the five presidential elections after the election of 1800, the nation's first two-party system gradually disappeared, as the Federalist Party disintegrated and the Republican Party became utterly dominant. It was so dominant that James Monroe would run for his second term as president in 1820 without facing any serious opposition. The times were nicknamed the Era of Good Feelings, and certainly they felt good to the triumphant Republicans, and were a relatively peaceful time for the nation. For a stretch of twenty-four years, or six elections, every president had been from Virginia, and each of Jefferson's successors had served as secretary of state to the man who had preceded him. The process ran like clockwork.

Such stability could not last forever, especially not in such a changing and ever-expanding country. The year 1824 would mark the point of departure into an entirely new kind of politics, coming out of a bitterly contested election.

The election would be fought out among four candidates, all of them Republicans: John Quincy Adams, Henry Clay, William Crawford, and the political outsider Andrew Jackson. The results were chaotic. Jackson seemed to have the most popular votes and electoral votes, but he did not have a majority of either. That meant that the House of Representatives would have to choose the president from among the top three candidates.

Henry Clay had been eliminated as the low vote getter. But he had great influence in the House and could use his influence to turn the vote in the direction of either Adams or Jackson (Crawford had to withdraw due to health problems). Clay chose Adams, which made possible Adams's narrow election; and then Clay was selected by Adams to be his secretary of state. Jackson and his followers were outraged! "Corrupt bargain!" they cried. The accusation seemed to stick with Adams for the next four years of what must be counted an unsuccessful presidency.

Adams himself was a remarkable man, as you might expect from the son of the second president. He was a man of aristocratic bearing, high morality, and superb intelligence who had been an outstanding secretary of state for James Monroe. Few men were better equipped for the presidency. But he had the misfortune to rise to the office at a moment when his own party was fracturing, and he lacked the personality and the political skill to adjust to the changing times.

He would be soundly defeated by Jackson in their 1828 rematch, by which time Jackson had rallied around himself a whole new political party, drawing on the surging energies of the West and South and the growing spirit of democratic equality in the land. Jackson called it the Democratic-Republican Party, but its name would soon become shortened to the Democratic Party, the ancestor of today's party of that same name.

It was an ugly campaign. Those running Adams's campaign mocked Jackson as an rude and ill-tempered brawler who was ignorant about the issues. The Jacksonians returned the favor by portraying Adams as a haughty aristocrat who had been corrupted by his time in the courts of Europe and who felt nothing but contempt for the common man. Jackson had the additional advantage of being a certifiable military hero, whose rise to glory had been part of the surge of American nationalism. His appeal to the common man had fit well with the rising influence of an ever-expanding electorate, broadening year by year to include more and more eligible voters – not just landholders but workers, artisans, tenant farmers, and others who had previously been excluded.

In a sense, the crudeness of the campaign and the enlarging of the electorate were related. Politics would be different in the Age of the Common Man. Previous campaigns had generally been restrained and respectable affairs, waged between candidates who were wellborn, refined, and educated. The broadening of the vote meant that politicians needed to find a way to appeal directly to relatively new voters who were new to the political process. The results were bound to be messy and somewhat undignified. Popular campaigning was often as much a matter of popular entertainment as of serious discussion of issues, with parades, marching bands, and rallies featuring free food and drink. The worst thing a candidate could do in the new era would be to come off as an aristocratic snob, as Adams often did.

The chaotic scene at Jackson's inauguration in Washington on March 4, 1829, was a good measure of how much things had changed. There were crowds of his rowdy, ill-mannered admirers lining Pennsylvania Avenue and later thronging into the White House, tracking mud on the rugs and standing on the chairs to get a glimpse of their man. And to be sure, Jackson was unlike any major candidate ever seen before in American presidential history.

He was a self-made, brawling, dueling, and tobacco-chewing frontiersman who had come from hard beginnings. He had risen through the ranks of society without the benefit of a college education to become a wealthy, accomplished, and powerful man, a national hero, while never losing his common touch, or his rough manners, or his ability to project sympathy for those of lower station. John Quincy Adams disparaged him as a "barbarian," but his many admirers begged to disagree.

This combination of traits not only suggests the breadth of his political appeal but points to one of the chief ways that Jacksonian democracy differed from Jeffersonian democracy. If Jefferson had believed that education could raise the commonest man to the same station as the wellborn, then Jackson believed that the common man was already where he needed to be and needed no raising. The common man had an inborn capacity for deciding questions of politics and economy on his own. A belief in that capacity was the trademark of genuine democracy. Indeed, Jackson can be said to be

America's first leader deserving of the title *populist,* meaning that opposition to (and resentment of) rule by privileged elite classes was one of the most important forces behind his political appeal.

In some ways, Jackson's symbolic significance as the representation of a new Age of the Common Man turned out to be more important than his presidency. He came into office without great plans, and much of his achievement was negative, meaning that he prevented things from happening: by his frequent use of the veto power (he vetoed more bills than all six of his predecessors combined), his firm rejection of the idea of nullification, meaning the ability of states to reject federal laws they didn't like (floated by South Carolina over a tariff dispute), and his relentless opposition to the rechartering of the Bank of the United States. He also, as we shall see, openly defied John Marshall's Supreme Court.

In many respects, his political instincts represented a throwback to Jefferson's views regarding strict construction of the Constitution and limited government. Jackson had a particularly strong objection to the alliance of government and business, which became clear with his his stubborn opposition to the Bank of the United States. But he was inconsistent, sometimes favoring internal improvements like the National Road and sometimes opposing them.

Jackson brought several interesting ideas to the presidency, however. He correctly identified the president as the only individual in the entire American system of constitutional government who could be said to be the representative of *all* of the people. He took that fact to mean that he also was meant to be the protector of the common man against the abusive power of the wealthy, powerful, and well connected. This was an important step in the further definition of the presidential office.

He also insisted upon the principle of "rotation" in staffing his administration. This approach flowed from his confidence in the natural abilities of the common man and his suspicion of would-be specialists and experts. It meant that the terms of officeholders would be strictly limited. Rotation in office would, he believed, ensure that the federal government did not develop a class of corrupt civil servants who were set apart from the people and could take advantage of their control of specialized knowledge.

Jackson also left his mark on Indian policy, and there the mark was more troubling. Jackson's inclusive democratic spirit did not extend to Native Americans, whom he regarded, as many western settlers did, with a mixture of fear and condescension, and whose claims to their homelands he flatly rejected. But he insisted that he did not hate them and sometimes adopted a paternalistic tone toward them, as if he were a father and they were children. He believed the best and most humane solution to the problem that these original inhabitants represented was to remove them from their homelands and resettle them in the lands west of the Mississippi River.

And it was done. In 1830, the Indian Removal Act was signed into law, and by 1835, most eastern tribes had relocated to the West, some forty-six thousand individuals. Later, in 1838, after Jackson's term of office had ended, the U.S. Army forced fifteen thousand Cherokees in Georgia to leave for the Oklahoma Territory, on a difficult and humiliating eight-hundred-mile trek along what became known as the Trail of Tears. Some four thousand died along the way.

It should be noted, too, that John Marshall suffered a notable setback in the matter of the Cherokee removal from Georgia, which he opposed. In the case *Worcester v. Georgia* (1832), the Court ruled that the laws of Georgia had no force within Cherokee territory. Jackson, however, sided with Georgia and simply ignored the ruling, thereby rendering it ineffective and futile. It was a powerful illustration of the limits of the Supreme Court's power when an executive is determined to reject its pronouncements.

A European traveler witnessed the effects of the Indian removal firsthand, as he happened by chance upon a group of Choctaws crossing the Mississippi River at Memphis in December 1831. That observer was the great French writer Alexis de Tocqueville (1805–59). He was deeply moved by what he saw.

"One cannot imagine the frightful evils that accompany these forced migrations," he remarked, and he went on to describe in compelling detail the frigid winter scene, the ground hardened with snow and enormous pieces of ice drifting down the river, as the Indian families gathered in silent and sorrowful resignation on the east bank of the river, proceeding without tears or complaints to cross over into what they knew to be an erasure of their past. It was, Tocqueville said, a "solemn spectacle that will never leave my memory."

Tocqueville, who would eventually become one of the most eminent European social and political thinkers of the nineteenth century, had come to America for completely different reasons. He was only twenty-six years old and almost completely unknown. Accompanied by his friend Gustave de Beaumont, he came to America intent upon "examining, in details and as scientifically as possible, all the mechanisms of the vast American society which everyone talks of and no one knows." The result, his two-volume book *Democracy in America* (1835–40), is perhaps the most enduring study of American society and culture ever written. It's often said that if you were permitted to read only one book on the subject, *Democracy in America* would almost certainly be your best choice – an astonishing statement, given the fact that nearly two centuries have passed since it was written and published.

As the earlier depiction of the Choctaw removal illustrates, Tocqueville did not excuse the moral defects of Jacksonian America. He was an objective foreign observer, not an American cheerleader. But his book also vividly captured the era's enterprising spirit and the energies that the democratic revolution in America was setting loose in the world.

Tocqueville saw the United States as a nation moving in the forefront of history, a young and vigorous country with an extraordinary degree of equality among its inhabitants, and with no feudal or aristocratic background in its past to overcome. In America, he believed, one could see the condition toward which all the rest of the world, including his native France, was going to be tending. In America, the world's only example of a large republic, one could gaze upon "the image of democracy itself, of its penchants, its character, its prejudices, its passions" – and, having so gazed, could perhaps take away lessons that would allow leaders to deal more intelligently and effectively with the democratic changes that were coming to Europe.

Tocqueville's portrait of America was of a strikingly middle-class society, full of ambitious, acquisitive, practical, equality-minded, and restlessly mobile people – a constant beehive of enterprise and activity. It was also a surprisingly religious society, in which the spirit of liberty and the spirit of religion were understood to be complimentary to one another, so that religious belief supported democratic practice – a totally different state of affairs from what he had found at home in France. Even though it was not to his personal taste, Tocqueville saw many things to admire in this brash and energetic democracy.

But he also saw some things to fear.

Chief among the dangers was America's pronounced tendency toward individualism. Tocqueville saw in America the peril that citizens might withdraw from involvement in public life and become isolated actors, with no higher goal than the pursuit of their own personal well-being.

But where, then, would the civic virtues needed for a decent society come from? What would become of the ideal of self-rule when no one was willing to take on the tasks of citizenship?

We may perhaps hear a faint echo in these questions of the Anti-Federalists' worries, and Jefferson's, about the fate of virtue in a commercial society filled with ambitious people who are too busy seeking their self-interest to give much thought to the common good. This was an issue that would not go away and is still with us today.

One thing was certain, though, and Tocqueville recognized it too. The Americans of Jackson's day were in the process of creating something new – not just a different kind of government but a different kind of culture. We'll turn to that next.

16 · THE CULTURE OF DEMOCRACY

In his classic account of democracy in America, Alexis de Tocqueville was interested in much more than just politics. He claimed that democracy influenced every facet of human life: not only public institutions but also family life, literature, philosophy, manners, language usage, marriage, friendship, love, and war. Democracy is a matter of culture, of a people's shared outlook and their way of life: their habits, convictions, morals, tastes, and spiritual life.

So what did this emerging culture of democracy look like in America?

The answer begins with a look at American religion as it developed in the years after the Revolution. The first thing to notice is that the remarkable partnership of Protestantism and the Enlightenment that we noticed in earlier times was beginning to come apart.

On the upper-class level, more and more of those in the established churches of the North found the Calvinist belief in natural human sinfulness to be too negative, out of touch with the steadily improving world that they saw emerging around them. They were drawn to more rational offshoots of Christianity, such as Deism and Unitarianism, both of which departed from standard Christian beliefs, stressing instead the innate goodness of human beings, along with their ability to improve their own lot in life by the exercise of their reason.

Some of the most important leaders of the Revolutionary generation, such as Jefferson and Franklin, had already been drawn in that direction, and in the early years of the new nation, rational approaches to religion grew in influence, although they always remained largely an upper-class taste. By the 1820s, Unitarianism had become the overwhelmingly predominant faith of the elite classes in Massachusetts and dominated the outlook at upper-class bastions like Harvard College.

But there was interesting activity taking place on the other side of the religious divide – the revivalist side. A Second Great Awakening had already begun in the years around 1800, led by men like Yale's president Timothy Dwight. He attempted to return that campus, which had declined, he said, into a "hotbed of infidelity," to something more like its intensely Puritan beginnings. A brilliant and charismatic speaker, Dwight led campus revivals that inspired many young Yale men to become evangelists.

Meanwhile, revivals on the southern and western frontiers were greater in number and far more lively. In fact, they tended to be raucous and emotional, to an extent that they were somewhat frightening to observers like Tocqueville, who referred to this revivalist spirit as "an exalted and almost fierce spiritualism." One such revival, a legendary camp meeting at Cane Ridge, Kentucky, in summer 1801, lasted for a week and attracted as many as twenty thousand people. It featured ecstatic and emotional outpourings from the many lonely and unchurched men and women of the frontier, who lived in poverty and isolation and yearned for spiritual uplift.

The ministers who worked on the frontier adapted their message to the circumstances. Instead of preaching complicated theology, they offered a simple message of personal salvation, easily grasped by anyone. Traveling revivals became a fixture of frontier life, and tireless Methodist "circuit riders," such as Francis Asbury and Peter Cartwright, provided a moveable evangelism in which the church came to the people themselves. Carrying only what they could fit in their saddlebags, the circuit riders were constantly on the move, riding through uncharted wilderness areas and small villages and conducting simple religious services wherever there was space for them. Cartwright, a man of astonishing stamina, delivered a sermon a day for more than twenty years, all the while riding a circuit on horseback that took in several states and presented all the rugged challenges and perils of frontier travel. The heroic efforts of Cartwright and others like him soon built Methodism into the largest Christian denomination in America.

By the 1820s, the currents of revivalism spread to upstate New York, in the region between Lake Ontario and the Adirondack Mountains, from Buffalo to Albany. It was the very region where the Erie Canal had been built, an area in which swift economic development had brought with it rapid changes in the pattern of life. Perhaps that is why the region showed such an unusual openness to spiritual things, becoming known as the "burned-over district" because of the frequency with which the flames of revival had swept through it.

It was there in 1821 that a young lawyer named Charles Grandison Finney underwent a "mighty baptism of the Holy Ghost" that enveloped him in "waves and waves of liquid love" and had come out of the experience with the clear conviction that he was to become an evangelist: "I have a retainer from the Lord Jesus Christ," he announced, sounding like a lawyer, "to plead his case." He immediately began to study to become a Presbyterian minister and by 1823 was ordained and began pleading the case in his unique way, using showmanship and simple theology to produce conversion after conversion among those in his audiences.

Finney was the greatest revivalist of his day, and his style became the basis for the modern American evangelical preacher, in the mold of Billy Graham and his stadium-sized open-air revivals during the twentieth century. Yet Finney's beliefs were different from those of Calvinism. He believed that the saving of souls did not have to wait upon grace; it was possible to cause conversion by the use of "new methods" designed to produce the proper emotional state and receptiveness. Finney was a master of the art, and using such techniques as the "anxious bench," where those called forward would publicly confess their sins and seek forgiveness, while surrounded by family and friends, he was able to transform his revivals into spectacular emotional experiences. When accused of manipulation, Finney simply replied that "the results justify my method."

Finney's theology and practices were a clear departure from established Christian doctrines. He showed little regard for the authority of the historic church and the clergy as essential parts of the Christian life. But such changes were an adjustment not only to the frontier but to a new democratic age. They reflected the optimism and individualism of the Jacksonian moment.

In a sense, Finney's transformation of Christianity into a positive creed of salvation that could be achieved through human exertion had a lot in common with the rational faith of the Unitarians. Both were setting aside the Calvinist emphasis on human sinfulness as something that didn't fit in with the rising confidence of the age. In certain respects, the two sides of America's religious divide were not as different as they might have seemed.

Finney's innovations were not the only ones in the burned-over district. That rapidly changing region was fertile ground for all kinds of ideas, even heretical ones, arising out of the spirit of the age. There were cults like the Millerites that preached the end of the world and the imminent establishment of God's Kingdom. There were those like the Fox sisters, who called themselves "spiritualists," and claimed the ability to communicate with the dead. There were radical social experiments in creating a utopia. There were intense efforts to recreate the purity of the early church.

Probably the most enduringly important of these innovations was the Church of Jesus Christ of Latter Day Saints, otherwise known as the Mormons. Today, some two centuries after the founding of Mormonism, we are unlikely to see this sturdy and conservative church as an expression of burned-over district religious radicalism. But it was.

It all began with a teenaged boy named Joseph Smith Jr., whose family had moved from Vermont to the small town of Palmyra,

New York. Smith believed he had experienced a series of supernatural visions, which led to his production, or discovery, of the Book of Mormon, a narrative account of certain ancient Hebrews who were said to have inhabited the New World and had an encounter with Jesus Christ. This book was thought of as an addition to the canon of Christian holy scripture – Smith regarded it as a lost section of the Bible – connecting the world of the Hebrew Bible with the original inhabitants of North America, and the current ones as well. In 1830, Smith began to form his own church, attracting converts by the dozens, and then hundreds, drawn to the church's new theology and its strong sense of community.

Like so many strains of Protestant Christianity, Mormonism reflected a desire to recover the purity of the early church. But its differences from the mainstream of Protestantism were striking. It understood God as a personal being, Jesus as his literal son, and the church as headed by a prophet who administered a male priesthood. While it accepted the Old and New Testaments of the Bible as sacred scriptures, it gave equal weight to the Book of Mormon and the revelations of the prophet. It envisioned human beings as ultimately aspiring not merely to eternal life but to the status of gods.

Above all else, Mormonism demanded of its members a very tightly organized community life, emphasizing a strong dedication to family, hard work, and personal discipline, including abstention from alcohol, tobacco, and drugs. There was a remarkable unity to Mormon community life, the strong sense of being a people apart, a "chosen" people like the Jews who had rejected the practices of the "gentiles" around them.

Mormonism showed the staying power to survive and thrive when so many of the other religious innovations of its era faded away. Yet its insistence upon strong and exclusive group bonds caused its members to clash with their neighbors. Matters were made far worse by Joseph Smith's adoption of the practice of "plural marriage," or polygamy, in which men were permitted to have more than one wife. That no doubt helped the sect grow more quickly, but it made the Mormons notorious, even hated, and probably ensured that the subsequent history of Mormonism in American history for much of the century would be one of nearly uninterrupted persecution. The Mormons moved from New York to Ohio to Illinois, but violence and hostility followed them wherever they went.

Finally, in 1844, after an anti-Mormon mob killed Joseph Smith and his brother Hyrum, they decided to leave the country for land in Utah, which was then part of Mexico. Led by Brigham Young, who would make a strong and highly intelligent successor to Smith, the entire community of fifteen thousand made the great trek to the Great Salt Lake basin, the "Promised Land," beginning in 1846. They arrived to find a desert, friendly to nothing but crickets and snakes. But they wasted no time in developing an irrigation system, which was in place by 1848. And then, putting their customary industriousness to work, they proceeded to make the desert bloom.

Mormonism was more than a religion. It also was an experimental community – and far from being the only important such experiment going on in America during these years. "We are all a little mad here with numberless projects of social reform," wrote Ralph Waldo Emerson in 1840. "Not a reading man but has a draft of a new community in his pocket." He exaggerated only slightly. There were more than a hundred utopian communities launched in the United States during the nineteenth century – not surprising in a country that was born (as we already saw in Chapter Three) with a burst of utopian thinking. A land of hope does not abandon its hopes so easily, even the wildest ones, and an optimistic and prosperous age was the perfect time for such experiments in living.

Some of those communities were short-lived. But others proved surprising durable, and the most durable ones generally had a strong religious dimension, as the Mormons had.

The Rappites, a group of German Lutherans who fled persecution and settled in Butler County, Pennsylvania, lasted until the end of the century, holding their possessions in common, advocating celibacy, and waiting for the second coming of Christ, which they believed was due to happen soon. Similarly, the Shakers, who believed God to be a dual personality, and believed their leader, Ann Lee Stanley, to be the second coming of Christ, lived lives of communal simplicity as brothers and sisters, joyfully anticipating that the fulfillment of the universe was near. Their movement flourished in the 1830s and 1840s and lasted into the twentieth century.

These utopian communities were signs of a culture that believed in the idea of reform and the unlimited possibilities for moral and spiritual transformation. As Emerson declared, writing in 1841, "In the history of the world the doctrine of Reform had never such scope as at the present hour ... and not a kingdom, town, statute, rite, calling, man, or woman, but is threatened by the new spirit." There was not only an embrace of the reshaping of society through disciplined communal living but also a strengthened commitment to the idea of a free public education for all young people and a keener awareness of and concern for society's forgotten or unrepresented, such as slaves, Native Americans, the laboring classes, women, children, and the disabled. Behind these rising ideals were the concept of human perfectibility and the confidence that the place and the moment for its pursuit had arrived in America, here and now.

Perhaps the most popular of all these causes was the temperance movement – the movement to limit, and ultimately abolish, the consumption of alcoholic beverages. This grew out of an optimistic belief in the possibility of achieving moral perfection but also addressed itself to a very real problem: the many negative effects of alcohol consumption on workers, families, and children. It has been estimated that in 1830, the average American over the age of fifteen consumed about three times what we consume today!

It is not hard to imagine the ill effects of such consumption on health, on worker safety and productivity, and on economic well-being. Drink, said a temperance pamphlet, was "the prolific source (directly or indirectly) of nearly all the ills that afflict the human family." In those days, it was not an unrealistic claim. A group of Boston ministers organized the American Society for the Promotion of Temperance to campaign for pledges of "total abstinence" –

those who took the pledge had a T by their names and were therefore called "teetotalers" – and ultimately for the restriction or prohibition of the sale of alcoholic beverages.

But there were plenty of other humanitarian causes. The expansion of women's rights was another area of growing interest, as women's roles in the workplace and in public life expanded beyond the strictly domestic sphere, and as women active in reform movements like temperance and antislavery became anxious to play a more equal role in policy decision-making and governance. The cruel and careless treatment of the mentally ill drew the attention of Dorothea Dix, a former schoolteacher who mounted a national campaign to publicize the problem and press for more humane treatment and facilities.

Public education for all, with a strong dose of moral instruction, was the goal of Horace Mann, secretary of the Massachusetts Board of Education. Higher education began to flourish, too, as a large number of small colleges were founded beginning in the 1830s by churches and religious groups. Thomas Gallaudet opened a school for the deaf in Connecticut and Samuel Gridley Howe a school for the blind in Massachusetts. Reform was buzzing and blooming everywhere.

But the greatest of all reform causes, and the one that eventually enveloped all the others, was the cause of antislavery. Opposition to slavery had grown steadily since the 1780s. It surfaced in the controversy over Missouri, and by the 1830s, when the movement finally began to come together, it was being pursued largely as a religious cause rather than a secular one – a grave and soul-imperiling national sin rather than a mere withholding of rights. The great revivals of the Second Great Awakening had awakened the nation's religious conscience about this social ill and demanded that it be eradicated.

That moral sharpening of the issue made any compromise with the defenders of slavery extremely difficult. This was particularly the case for those who were called abolitionists, who actively sought the end of slavery. The leading abolitionists, such as William Lloyd Garrison, publisher of the abolitionist newspaper called the *Libera-*

tor and a fervent Quaker, were nearly all evangelical Protestants of some sort. Few were as radical as Garrison, however, a forceful and steel-spined man who demanded "immediate" emancipation and publicly burned a copy of the Constitution and condemned it as a "proslavery" document, a "Covenant with Death," and "an Agreement with Hell." Others were willing to work for gradual emancipation, carried out through existing political institutions. The great black abolitionist Frederick Douglass, himself a former slave and a former follower of Garrison, came to support that more gradual position.

The distinction matters. Some scholars have argued that the antislavery movement, particularly in its Garrisonian form, made things worse rather than better by increasing southern fears and pushing away more moderate northern allies. Others argue that, without abolitionists taking a strong and righteous position challenging the practice of slavery, and insisting upon its incompatibility with American and Christian beliefs, nothing would have changed and the nation would have just drifted forward, with the moral contradiction of slavery still unaddressed. This is a debate worth having, since it connects in some way to the complexity of almost every great moral cause in human history. Which voices are most deserving of our honor and our imitation?

The German sociologist Max Weber made a distinction between two ways of thinking about ethics and morality that we may find helpful in thinking about this question. He distinguished between the ethic of moral conviction and the ethic of responsibility, two different ways of thinking about how leaders address moral problems in politics.

The ethic of moral conviction was what propelled Garrison. It says that one must be true to one's principles and do the right thing, no matter what the cost and no matter what the consequences and side effects may be. It has a purity about it that is admirable. But is it realistic or wise?

The ethic of responsibility took a different view. It guided moderates (and, as we shall see, Abraham Lincoln himself) to the belief

that leaders have to take responsibility for the totality of effects arising out of their actions. One can do the right thing at the wrong
time, in the wrong way, and do an immense amount of damage to
good and innocent people in the process. It is not enough to say
that one's intentions are pure. One has to act in a way that produces
more good effects than bad. Such a distinction does not decide the
question, but it does clarify it.

But one more thing remains to be pointed out. Logic and reasoning are not always the things that change minds. One of the
chief forces that shifted northern public opinion about slavery was
not a treatise or a sermon or a speech or a work of political theory.
It was a work of fiction: Harriet Beecher Stowe's novel *Uncle Tom's
Cabin; or, Life among the Lowly*, published in 1852, which became
the best-selling American novel of the nineteenth century. Stowe
used the novel to depict the life of its title character, a slave who
was sold by his owner and torn from his family, but who retained
his loving spirit and Christian decency through a horrendous
sequence of cruel and violent acts eventuating in his death. The
book left a permanent impression on all who read it.

The book succeeded not because of its preaching on questions
of principle but because it appealed, vividly and emotionally, to
Americans' sense that no institution could be defended if it violated
the sanctity of the family. It succeeded because it endowed its black
characters with undeniable dignity and brought the reader to iden-
tify with their suffering, and to feel the injustice of it. And it succeeded all the more because it showed that one of the worst aspects
of slavery was its degrading effect upon the master class itself. In
other words, it demonstrated the wrongness of the institution by
vividly showing its awful consequences to *everyone* involved in it.

There is an important lesson in this for us, today. We should
never underestimate the power of the imagination, and its role in
making history.

17 · THE MAKING OF AN AMERICAN LITERATURE

$\mathbf{A}$MERICA HAD GOOD REASON to be proud of its political institutions. They were, for all their faults, the freest and most democratic in the world. But there was a lingering question as to whether that success could also occur in the realm of literature and the arts. Could America ever produce a *high* culture that was as fresh, distinctive, and admirable as its political institutions? Could it produce its own art, literature, music, drama, and architecture that could stand comparison to the similar products of Europe?

Tocqueville was skeptical. Looking at the literary culture of the country, he was unimpressed. He noticed that Americans seemed only to read English books, rather than books by their own authors, and speculated that the longer-run effect of democracy on literature would be to foster mediocrity. There would be many small-scale works, written with the marketplace in mind, often gimmicky or sensational, tailored for a busy and practical-minded people, but nothing great or enduring.

His attitude was a milder version of the disdain expressed by the British literary critic Sidney Smith, writing in the *Edinburgh Review* in 1820, when he posed these questions "In the four quarters of the globe, who reads an American book? or goes to an American play? or looks at an American picture or statue?" The answer was obvious to him: nobody did.

As harsh as such words may sound, they had some truth to them. In the years before 1830, only James Fenimore Cooper managed to find a literary vein to work in his Leatherstocking tales that reflected the drama of life on the American frontier, with memorable characters like the brave and resourceful frontier scout Natty Bumppo, who had been raised by Delaware Indians. In addition to Cooper, the melancholy southern writer Edgar Allan Poe, whose weird mystery tales, detective fiction, and literary criticism were far ahead of his time, would be read with respect overseas. So, too, was Washington Irving, whose colorful fables about Rip Van Winkle and Sleepy Hollow won him a moment of fame abroad. But there were few, if any, others.

By the 1830s, that was beginning to change, as American writers started to find their voice and as the elements of a distinctive American culture began to come into being. By the 1850s, a big breakthrough had taken place. How and why did that happen?

A good way to begin thinking about American literature and art in this time is to stress the tremendous influence of the European romantic movement in the realm of ideas, literature, and the arts. *Romanticism* is a complex term, very hard to define. It fact, it's often easier to say what romanticism is against rather than what it is for.

But we can say this much: Romanticism was in rebellion against a tidy and rational view of the world that makes no room for emotion, mystery, spontaneity, imagination, fantasy, creativity, or the deepest and most inexpressible needs of the soul. Although it began in Europe, it found a very welcoming environment in America. Many of the key ideas associated with romanticism – the emphasis upon the individual, the love of nature, the distrust of civilization and the love of the primitive – sound like elements of the Jacksonian era's popular culture.

But romantic ideas made their greatest impact in America through the works of a few people, a circle of thinkers who were very much a product of the religious and intellectual culture of New England, at a particular moment, in a particular place.

And I do mean a very *particular* place. A century and half ago, peaceful little Concord, Massachusetts, outside Boston, was a hub of the American literary and cultural universe. One could hardly think of a more illustrious circle of American writers than Ralph Waldo Emerson, Nathaniel Hawthorne, Henry David Thoreau, Bronson Alcott, and Margaret Fuller. All of them knew one another, lived in or near Concord at roughly the same time, and wrote many of their most important works there. Indeed, all of them (with the exception of Fuller, who died in a shipwreck) are also buried there today. There is perhaps no single location in all of American literary history that matters more, and was more alive with the sense of possibility.

These writers shared a fascination with a cluster of ideas and ideals that go under the name of Transcendentalism, a romantic outlook that stressed the glories of Nature while placing the ideal of the majestic Self at the center of its thought, and at the center of Nature also. It had no respect for tradition or other older sources of authority and wisdom. The past was raw material to be fed upon selectively, with only the needs of the present in view. It also was suspicious of "society," which Emerson dismissed as a "conspiracy against the manhood of every one of its members," and was deeply distrustful of all social movements, even those for undeniably good causes. Instead, it placed emphasis on the power and strength of the individual.

Although Transcendentalism had nothing to do with popular forms of Christianity, it resembled evangelicalism in one important way. It sought to overthrow the established authority of social elites and to ground religion in the authority of individual experience. Each person would know for himself or herself. As such, then, Transcendentalism can be understood as part of the expansive, hopeful, experimental, and sometimes utterly bizarre spirit of antebellum American reform – a moment when some Americans seemed ready to reconsider *everything*, all existing social arrangements.

The establishment against which Transcendentalism was rebelling was Unitarianism, which was itself an intellectually liberal (though politically conservative) rebellion against old-line Calvinism. Emerson himself was the offspring of a long line of ministers in that tradition, including his Unitarian minister father William, whom Emerson followed into the Unitarian ministry.

But discontent with Unitarianism finally led him, in 1832, to resign his position at Boston's prestigious Second Church, even without any clear notion of what was to come next. After a period of travel in Europe, he resolved to set himself up as an independent writer and speaker. His efforts would gain support from the growing public interest in self-improvement and unconventional religious and spiritual explorations.

A critical moment in his development was his delivery in 1837 of the annual Phi Beta Kappa address at Harvard, a challenging, occasionally taunting speech which would become known as "The American Scholar" and which would finally launch him in his newly conceived role. The speech was a plea for American cultural independence and originality, a challenge to the rationalism of Harvard, and a life plan for passionately independent minds like his own. "The American Scholar" would become one of the most celebrated academic lectures in American history. Read how it concludes:

> *Mr. President and Gentlemen, this confidence in the unsearched might of man, belongs by all motives, by all prophecy, by all preparation, to the American Scholar. We have listened too long to the courtly muses of Europe. The spirit of the American freeman is already suspected to be timid, imitative, tame.... Not so, brothers and friends, please God, ours shall not be so. We will walk on our own feet; we will work with our own hands; we will speak our own minds.... A nation of men will for the first time exist, because each believes himself inspired by the Divine Soul which also inspires all men.*

One observer referred to "The American Scholar" as America's declaration of *intellectual* independence, and the comparison was very fitting. Emerson saw the American Revolution as a beacon to all of humanity and believed that the embattled farmers of his beloved Concord had indeed fired "the shot heard round the world," in the words of his own patriotic poem called "Concord Hymn" – probably the best-known words Emerson ever wrote. Hence, when he called for Americans to cease taking their cues from "the courtly muses of Europe," he was not saying it should withdraw from the larger world. He was urging that America find its own voice at last.

That was a principle that Emerson also saw reflected in individual life. See for example the swaggering energy of these words from his 1841 essay "Self-Reliance":

> *Whoso would be a man, must be a non-conformist. He who would gather immortal palms must not be hindered by the name of goodness, but must explore if it be goodness.*
>
> *No law can be sacred to me but that of my nature. Good and bad are but names very readily transferable to that or this; the only right is what is after my constitution; the only wrong what is against it.*
>
> *The great man is he who in the midst of a crowd keeps with perfect sweetness the independence of solitude.*
>
> *Ah, then, exclaim the aged ladies, you shall be sure to be misunderstood! Misunderstood! It is a right fool's word. Is it so bad then to be misunderstood? Pythagoras was misunderstood, and Socrates and Jesus, and Luther, and Copernicus, and Galileo, and Newton, and every pure and wise spirit that ever took flesh. To be great is to be misunderstood.*

Yes, there is brag and swagger in these words. But they also are very American words.

So, too, were Emerson's entirely different words in the Harvard speech, calling for a new understanding of ordinary life, one that reflected a very democratic outlook. "I ask not for the great, the remote, the romantic," he wrote; "I explore and sit at the feet of the familiar, the low." Instead of the elite European emphasis upon the doings of heroes and kings and queens and aristocrats, he pleaded for something new: a literature that exalts the common people and things that the courtly muses had never lowered themselves to take notice of, a literature "of the poor, the feelings of the child, the philosophy of the street, the meaning of household life." Emerson's idea of democratic culture could include both the grandeur of the free mind and a tender respect for the ordinary details of everyday existence. He saw no contradiction between the two.

Others in the Concord circle who felt Emerson's influence also became influential in their own right. Henry David Thoreau, who was Emerson's neighbor and something of a follower, tried to put Emerson's ideas of self-reliance to the test spending over two years living alone in a cabin on Walden Pond, devoting most of his time to reflection and writing. Out of that experience of enforced simplicity and economy came one of the finest books in the American literary tradition, his *Walden; or, Life in the Woods*, a blend of spiritual reflection, hard-edged social criticism, and keen observation of nature. Thoreau announced his intentions with these opening words: "I went to the woods because I wished to live deliberately, to front only the essential facts of life, and see if I could not learn what it had to teach, and not, when I came to die, discover that I had not lived." Going back to the essentials of nature: what could be more American?

Nathaniel Hawthorne was also a product of the same circle, even if in some ways a dissenting participant. During his student days at Bowdoin College, he had become friendly with classmate Henry Wadsworth Longfellow, and after hearing Longfellow's 1825 commencement address, "Our Native Writers," he had been afire with the idea of realizing the dream of creating a truly American literature. His 1850 novel *The Scarlet Letter* was a breakthrough, the first great American novel, a work that would be read and respected the world over. He shared an enthusiasm for many aspects of the romantic rebellion, questioning the scientific world-view and delighting in stories that were full of supernatural and uncanny elements.

But Hawthorne dissented from the hopefulness of the others. Instead, he stalked the era's official optimism like a shadowy gray ghost, propelled by a spirit of inherited Puritan skepticism. His early stories, collected as *Twice-Told Tales* (1837), made use of the New England past to explore issues of sin and guilt, the issue to which he brought a master's touch in *The Scarlet Letter*, a penetrating analysis of a Puritan community's sinfully cruel treatment of an act of adultery. He wrote his novel *Blithedale Romance* (1852) as a put-down of the utopian delusions behind the Brook Farm experiment in communal living, in which he had participated. His entire literary output can be thought of as a stern and consistent scolding to the giddy optimism of his age and the false hopes and hidden terrors it failed to recognize. And yet he, too, was very American: as American as Emerson, as American as the Puritans.

Although a New Yorker by birth and only indirectly a member of the Concord circle, Herman Melville was a friend and admirer, to the point of adoration, of Nathaniel Hawthorne. It was under the influence of Hawthorne that he took the fateful turn in his writing that led him to produce *Moby-Dick* (1851), arguably the greatest of all American novels. That sprawling drama of the voyage of the whaling ship *Pequod* in search of the Great White Whale. under the direction of the mad and relentless Captain Ahab. was based upon Melville's experience. He had gone to sea as a young man – "a whale ship was my Yale College and my Harvard," he said – and learned much about the extremes of life. On one voyage to the South Sea islands, he jumped ship, had many adventures, was captured by cannibals, participated in a mutiny, and came home with a huge treasury of stories and experiences. He drew on this treasury for a series of novels that were commercial successes but not especially memorable or enduring.

Then, after meeting Hawthorne, he changed his objectives as a writer, and the result was *Moby-Dick*, a stunning masterpiece in which everything from the anatomy of whales to the existence of God is up for discussion. Unfortunately, Melville drove off his sea-yarn-loving audience. *Moby-Dick* became a commercial failure, and it sank like a stone, remaining forgotten for the next seventy years, until it would be rediscovered by scholars.

Finally, the 1850s saw the emergence of the poet Walt Whitman, who is arguably the most Jacksonian American writer of all. Unlike the Concord circle, he was a man of the city who adored the jagged contours and bustling crowds of the modern Brooklyn and Manhattan and wrote poetry about riding the ferry between them. There was not an ounce of snobbery in him, and he enjoyed mingling with all kinds of people, from the roughest street toughs to the upper-class audiences at grand opera houses. He worked for years as an editor for newspapers in Brooklyn, New York, and New Orleans, signing his material as "Walter" Whitman and showing little of the astoundingly original literary flair that would become his trademark. He had, however, read Emerson, and when his first book, *Leaves of Grass*, appeared in 1855, he sent it to Emerson, who hailed it as "the most extraordinary piece of wit and wisdom that America has yet contributed."

The front of the book featured a picture of Whitman dressed in worker's clothing, with his undershirt visible and his hat cocked at an angle. He was, he went on, "not a bit tamed – I too am untranslatable; / I sound my barbaric yawp over the roofs of the world." Writing in free unrhymed verse, using uncustomary and even startling images – the odors and passions of the body, the occupations of bricklayers and housekeepers – he presented all of reality as equally worthy of his attention, the ultimate democracy of the mind and heart and spirit.

At times, it could all seem like a mess, and Whitman, too, took many years to find his proper audience. He was, and is, easy to make fun of. But the British writer and critic D. H. Lawrence recogized in Whitman an achievement going beyond the literary, expressing the emerging culture of democracy, not only as it was, but as it could be, better than anyone else had yet done:

Whitman's essential message was the Open Road. The leaving of the soul free unto herself, the leaving of his fate to her and to the loom of the open road. Which is the bravest doctrine man has ever proposed to himself.... The true democracy, where soul meets soul, in the open road.

It is, finally, a message of human dignity, of the infinite worth of the single and individual soul. Whitman's work expressed the deepest hopes of the age it represented.

18 · THE OLD SOUTH AND SLAVERY

IT IS HARD TO SAY exactly when "the South" became a distinct region within the new nation. Regional tensions over slavery were already evident, as we have seen, at the Constitutional Convention in 1787. But they were not that much greater than East–West tensions over other issues, and certainly not strong enough to compete with the desire to establish a strong national union. Indeed, you will recall that the earliest serious movements in the direction of state secession from the Union didn't come from the South. They came from New England, as in the case of the Hartford Convention.

All but two of the first seven presidents of the nation were southerners, a fact that did not cause alarm to the rest of the nation. Yes, regional tensions flared up over tariffs, which tended to favor northern industrial and commercial interests over southern agricultural ones. But it may not have been until Jefferson's "fire bell in the night," the 1819–21 crisis over the admission of Missouri to the Union, that the extent of the division – and the role of slavery in producing that division – became clear.

But the South had a certain unifying uniqueness. At the bottom of it all was a certain combination of climate and economics. Farming had been the basis of the southern economy from the time that tobacco was discovered and continued to be well into the nineteenth century. The South's climate was warm and humid, and the region enjoyed an almost year-round growing season, along with being equipped with numerous waterways for easy transportation.

All of these things made it ideal territory for the cultivation of cash crops, such as cotton, tobacco, rice, sugar, and indigo, which could be exported as a source of income.

By the early 1800s, there could be no doubt which of these crops was the most profitable and most important. By the 1850s, cotton accounted for two-thirds of all U.S. exports and linked together the South's growing agricultural economy with Great Britain's domination of the textile industry. The cultivation of such crops in large quantities required a continuing supply of vast tracts of land, and an equally large supply of inexpensive labor to do the backbreaking work that such large-scale agriculture required. As a result, pressures to expand westward were relentless. The plantation system and the institution of slavery were well suited to the mass production that such agriculture needed. They became central features of southern life.

The South also was a more self-contained area, more drawn in upon itself, more conscious of its own identity – and increasingly aware of its potential minority status within the growing nation. Unlike the North, it did not attract great waves of immigration from Europe, such as the influx of Irish and German refugees who streamed into northern cities during the 1840s. Instead, as the South became ever-more committed to slave labor to make its agricultural economy possible, it became less attractive to immigrants. This turned into a self-reinforcing cycle. The region's population grew slowly, and mainly from internal sources.

Thus the South became a strikingly biracial society, with stark differences of power and status – although strangely, underneath it all, there was also a certain commonality of culture. This is a contradiction not easily explained, although it may well have to do with the way that certain characteristics of agricultural life were shared across class and racial lines. Also, aside from south Louisiana, which retained much of its Catholic character, the population of the South was almost entirely Protestant in its religion. In any event, the amount of exchange and interchange between and among white and black southerners, in speech patterns, foodways, music, worship, folklore, and literary expression, was enormous – even despite the barriers of race, and the huge inequities of power and status.

Yet, at the same time, the mounting economic importance of slavery led, little by little, to a stiffening determination among some southern whites to defend their "peculiar institution," as they came to call slavery. This was true even though, even at the height of the institution, only a minority of southern whites were slave owners, and only a tiny number of those were plantation owners with large numbers of slaves under their command.

This would lead to grave consequences. As the historian U. B. Phillips put it, "the central theme" of southern history became the "common resolve" that the white population should maintain its dominance. Such unity would, however, be purchased at a fearful price – a price that would be paid by enslaved black southerners.

The Old South was an overwhelmingly agricultural society, then, in which the production and sale of cotton was the single most important element in the economy. Cities were few and far between, and there was not much economic activity beyond agriculture. It was also a very wealthy region, but the wealth was concentrated in a very few hands. The wealthy were perched atop a very perilous social and economic structure. They were ultimately dependent upon the price of cotton and the use of forced labor for their lofty standing. That perch proved to be an unstable one.

Cotton was sought after all over the world, and especially in Great Britain, where southern cotton became the force powering the British textile industry. That success made the planter class confident – overly confident – about their standing and their prospects. As world demand for cotton continued to rise, the South's future prosperity seemed assured. It even began to seem, to some, as if the southern economy could dictate its terms to the rest of the world. As the South Carolina planter James Henry Hammond boasted, if the South were to choose to deprive England of a steady supply of southern cotton, "England would topple headlong and carry the whole civilized world with her.... No, you dare not make war on cotton. No power on earth dares to make war upon it. Cotton is king."

Such words smacked of hubris, the excessive pride that goes before a fall. This mistaken confidence would lead to cruel and tragic consequences for the South. Lulled into a false sense of economic security by the illusion that cotton prices would never fall, the South would become fatally committed to a brutal social and economic system. That system was designed for the production of cotton on a massive scale, but it achieved such productivity at an vast human and moral cost. It placed the region on a collision course with fundamental American ideals.

The system was not a machine, however. It evolved into a complex and many-faceted way of life, whose contours would be as varied as the South itself. As has already been pointed out, the elite planter class was small in number, making up only about 4 percent of the adult white males in the South, and only a relative handful of those planters (around twenty-three hundred of them) owned at least one hundred slaves. The majority of slaveholders were ordinary farmers who owned fewer than twenty slaves and worked in the fields with them.

The majority of whites, three-fourths of them, were not slaveholders at all. They could not afford the rich, low-lying farmland favored by the planters and lived instead in the areas farther inland, getting their living largely as subsistence farmers, which meant that they grew enough to survive but not enough to create a surplus. Yet the large planters set the tone for the whole, exercising a huge influence on their societies and the legislatures of their states. Far from resenting them or begrudging them their wealth, most poor whites hoped someday to be able to follow in their footsteps.

Dominated as it was by an aristocratic planter class, the Old South in some ways resembled a feudal society, with all the strict social order that implies. Over time, the resemblance became increasingly self-conscious and was embraced by those at the top of the social pyramid.

Their vision was a variation on a very old theme: the belief that there is a "great chain of being" that links and orders all things, from the highest to the lowest, and that a society's harmony and well-being derive from its observing of that order.

But the trouble was that such a vision contradicted the idea that all men are equal in the eyes of the Creator. Nor was it compatible with the individualism and enterprise that Tocqueville had observed in America, a land where all individuals could strive to improve their lot in life and to rise in the world.

How had the South diverged from those ideals so widely, in such a short period of time? In later years, the writer Mark Twain claimed that books like Sir Walter Scott's 1820 historical romance *Ivanhoe*, which glorified the world of medieval England, had been the cause of the American Civil War, by filling the southern mind with "dreams and phantoms" of a "long-vanished society."

The claim was wild and farfetched, but there was a kernel of truth in it. The divergence of the antebellum South was not just a matter of differences over economics and politics. Such differences were upheld by contrasting social ideals. By the time the sectional conflict came to a head in the 1850s and 1860s, the extent of these cultural differences would make political compromise even more difficult.

Twain's observation conveyed another truth: "the South" was not only the South of the planter class. Nor was it merely the South of white people. By the middle of the nineteenth century, the institution of slavery was so completely inseparable from the southern way of life that it was impossible to consider southern culture apart from it. Black southerners, most of whom were enslaved, were a massive presence in southern life, from the very beginning, and exerted a constant influence on the culture of the South. To see the South whole means telling their story also.

That is not a simple matter. For one thing, the practice of slavery in North America was resistant to easy generalizations. Slavery in North America had begun as something approaching a casual afterthought, not always clearly distinct from indentured servitude. As it spread, it changed and adapted to circumstances. For the century and a half of British colonial rule, it existed as a system of forced or coerced labor that had not been thoroughly defined and codified, a feature of "benign neglect" with a wide and informal variety in the way it was practiced – and it was practiced in *all* the colonies, New England as well as the South. After the Revolution, however, it became localized to the South, as the northern states gradually abolished it.

Yet even after these changes had taken place, the working and living conditions of slavery could still vary dramatically, depending on the time and place – and the cruelty or kindness of individual masters. The living conditions of slaves on small farms in states like Kentucky in the Upper South, where they often found themselves living more like hired hands and working beside their masters in the fields, were very different from life on the giant sugar and cotton plantations of Louisiana and Alabama in the Deep South, where hundreds and even a thousand or more slaves were living and laboring together, confined under strict and often oppressive discipline.

The plantations formed complex slave mini-societies, with intricate divisions of labor and gradations of rank and status. At the top of the slave pecking order were the household servants and skilled workers, who worked in more refined circumstances, coming into contact frequently with the planter's family and generally having better quarters and better treatment. At the bottom were the field hands, who worked at backbreaking labor from dawn to dusk, sleeping in crude wooden shacks with dirt floors, poorly fed, poorly clothed and ill-shod, dwelling always in fear of the master's punitive lash.

Wherever there were larger concentrations of slaves, there one would also find surviving elements of African cultural and religious practices, often appearing as adaptations of the distinct African tribal cultures from which the slaves had originally come. The slaves' religion took on a distinctive flavor, blending Christianity with enthusiastic music and ecstatic African elements in ways that would come to distinguish much of African American worship in the years to come.

Their attraction to Christianity did not come solely out of obedience. Slaves found that many of the stories of the Bible spoke directly to their condition, in ways that their masters did not perceive. They especially took heart from the story of the Israelites' exodus from slavery in Egypt – just as John Winthrop and the Puritans had taken heart, two centuries before – seeing it as another version of their own tribulations and sufferings, sustaining their hope of eventual freedom. They could see their condition and their hopes mirrored in the humility of Jesus Christ, the God who came into the world in the guise of a lowly, suffering servant, who took the side of the poor and oppressed of the world and proved himself more powerful even in his earthly humiliation that anything that the existing authorities could do to him. His example gave them heart.

Religion was at the center of slaves' communal life. It was the thing that made it possible for them to sustain communities and families at all. The forces against their doing so were enormous, especially in the closed circumstances of the large plantations. Slave marriages had no legal validity, and no protections against the invasive force of the slave market, which dictated that families could be torn apart at any moment by an owner's decision to sell a husband, a wife, or (more often) a child. Ironically, the end of the legal slave trade in 1808 made such transactions more frequent, since the offspring of existing slaves had become even more valuable.

The immense sadness and longing one hears in the great spiritual songs that came out of the African American slave experience – songs like "Sometimes I Feel Like a Motherless Child" and "Nobody Knows the Trouble I've Seen" – were cries of the heart, products of that crucible of harsh and near-hopeless circumstances.

But those were not the only such products. There were also songs of exuberance and joy, such as "Rock My Soul in the Bosom of Abraham." And there were songs hinting at the possibility of this-worldly deliverance, such as "Steal Away to Jesus" and "Go Down, Moses," the latter of which was used by the black abolitionist Harriet Tubman as a coded signal to slaves thinking of fleeing to the North. Such songs, and the profound religious assurances that lay behind them, gave slaves the capacity to resist being completely overwhelmed by the circumstances of near-total domination in which they found themselves.

The slave religion taught the same lesson that many previous generations of Christians had learned: the soul can remain free even when the body is bound. While it would be wrong to minimize the psychological ravages of slavery, it would be equally wrong to deny the heroism and resiliency that slaves showed, guarding their hearts and keeping hope alive under hopeless conditions.

They resisted in outward ways too. Some of their methods were "day-to-day" acts of passive or indirect resistance: work slowdowns, feigned illness, deliberate sabotage, breaking of farming implements, setting fire to buildings, and a range of other acts of obstruction. Slaves' opportunities for escape were few and risky, and large-scale insurrections were all but suicidal. But some were willing to try, and others were willing to help. The ingenuity and courage of Tubman and other committed abolitionists created the Underground Railroad, an informal network of secret routes and safe houses sheltering and aiding escaped slaves seeking freedom in the North.

But those valiant efforts made only a small dent in the slave population of the South; and organized slave rebellions in the South were rare, and never successful. The example of the successful slave uprising in the 1790s in the French Caribbean island of Saint-Domingue (Haiti), which led to the murder or forced exile of thousands of former masters, had made a permanent impression upon the minds of Southern slaveholders. They were not about to permit something similar to happen on their soil.

There were only three major slave rebellions attempted in

nineteenth-century America, and only one of them, the Nat Turner Rebellion in Southampton County, Virginia, in August 1831, managed to move from plan to action. But that one rebellion, the bloodiest in American history, would have vast consequences.

Turner was a black overseer who was also a religious zealot, driven by prophetic visions to imagine that he was divinely ordained to lead a slave uprising. On August 22, 1831, Turner set out to do just that. He was accompanied by about seventy armed slaves and free blacks, united around the intention of slaughtering as many as possible of the white neighbors who enslaved them.

They began with Turner's master and his wife and children, hacking them to death with axes, and then went on to successive farmhouses, repeating the process until, by the end of the next day, they had killed around sixty whites: men, women, and children, bodies thrown into bonfires or left for the wolves. They were subdued the following day by the white militia, although Turner himself eluded capture for more than two months. In the end, the state executed fifty-six blacks and banished others; many more were killed by the militia without trial.

The ferocity of the Nat Turner Rebellion and its brutal suppression dramatically altered the mental and moral climate of the South. It sent chills of terror down the spines of white southerners, as rumors traveled far and wide about other such rebellions under way or in the making. There also were reports of violent white retaliation against blacks all over the South. Bloody violence was in the air; the civil order itself seemed threatened.

There was a sense that a great divide was being crossed – or perhaps had already been crossed. The rebellion occurred just as the abolition movement in the North was gathering steam – Garrison's the *Liberator* published its first issue in 1831 – making its appeal on the basis of Christian moral values that southerners generally shared. And yet, it occurred at a moment when the South's investment in slavery as an economic institution seemed to have become too great to abandon. They still were holding the wolf by the ear, as Thomas Jefferson had said a decade before.

Shortly afterward, at the 1831–32 session of the Virginia General Assembly, the state's legislators engaged in a far-reaching debate. It was occasioned by a flurry of some forty petitions, urging them to address the problems associated with slavery. This would be arguably the South's only full and free general debate over the status of the peculiar institution, and its tone was surprisingly critical.

Some called for outright emancipation, others for colonization, but none called for the protection of "perpetual slavery." Interestingly, although the delegates were divided about means, they did not differ about ends. All saw Virginia's future as lying with the free states to the north but differed only in the speed with which that end should be sought. None defended slavery in abstract terms; in fact, their compromise resolution did not hesitate to call slavery an evil, and they agreed that slavery would eventually end in Virginia.

After vigorous debate, the members narrowly rejected, by a vote of seventy-three to fifty-eight, a plan for gradual emancipation and African colonization, proposed by a descendant of Thomas Jefferson. Instead, members declined to pass any such laws, deciding instead that they "should await a more definite development of public opinion."

That decision doomed to failure any hope that slavery would be abandoned in an orderly and peaceable way. The window of opportunity for any such enlightened action was closing, and public opinion in the state was already running in the opposite direction. In fact, pro-slavery and anti-abolitionist opinion rapidly overtook the alternatives in the years that followed.

The General Assembly went on to pass legislation making it unlawful to teach slaves, free blacks, or mulattoes to read or write and restricting all blacks from holding religious meetings without the presence of a licensed white minister. Other slaveholding states across the South enacted similar laws restricting activities of slaves and free blacks. The institution of slavery was henceforth going to be even more closed, more devoted to total control, more bottled up, and more toxic than before. There was to be no loosening of the white South's uncomfortable grip on the wolf's ear.

Changes in ideas followed these changes in circumstances. The Turner revolt had forcefully exploded the wistful myths about the harmonious benevolence of slavery. But it did so at a moment when the South's dependency on its peculiar institution seemed too great and too thoroughly rooted to be abandoned – and at the very moment when the voices of northern abolitionists, although few in number and limited in influence, had suddenly become loud and threatening to southern slaveholders' ears.

A defense had to be mounted. But how could one make a robust defense of an institution that one also regarded as an evil on the way to gradual extinction? Would it not be more effective if southerners were to steel their minds and hearts for the struggle ahead with the firm belief that this indispensable institution was actually a positive good, and not merely a necessary evil?

Hence the emergence of an unapologetically "pro-slavery" argument.

In the view of the Virginian George Fitzhugh, perhaps the most influential of the pro-slavery writers, the institution of slavery was far preferable to the "wage slavery" of northern industrial society, in which greedy, profit-oriented capitalists took no responsibility for the well-being of their workers but instead exploited them freely and then cast them aside like used tissues when their labor was no longer useful.

Fitzhugh argued that free labor and free markets and other individual liberties only served to enrich the strong while crushing the weak. "Slavery," he wrote, "is a form, and the very best form, of socialism," the best counter to the rampant competitiveness of "free" societies. With Fitzhugh, we have come a very long way from the ideals of the American founders.

How many people really accepted such a radical and unvarnished version of the pro-slavery argument? That is hard to know. What is clearer, though, is that the pro-slavery argument's appearance on the scene, replacing the more complex "necessary evil" argument in the minds of many elite leaders, including such powerful men as the influential South Carolina politician John C. Calhoun, was a very bad sign for the future. It was a sign that the South was in the process of cutting itself off from the rest of the nation, and from the nation's shared political heritage, all to protect its "peculiar institution."

In many other ways, ranging from the seizure of the mails to prevent the entry of abolitionist literature into the South to the imposition of a "gag rule" in the U.S. House of Representatives to suppress any discussion relating to slavery and abolition, the southern states seemed intent upon taking off the table, once and for all, any and all reconsideration of slavery, and especially of the moral and political acceptability of slavery. The kind of open and frank discussion that took place in the Virginia General Assembly in 1831–32 had, almost overnight, become impossible.

How rapidly things had changed. No one had spoken positively of slavery in those earlier Virginia debates. Now it had become dangerous to speak of it in any other way. This change, this defensive hardening of southern opinion, was an omen of things to come, none of them good.

19 · A GATHERING STORM

WAS A CIVIL WAR between the North and South inevitable? Maybe so. It's hard for us today, over a century and a half later, to imagine things happening otherwise. We come to this drama already knowing the plot and knowing where it's leading.

But that habit of mind should be resisted, if we are truly to enter into the spirit of the past. History is very rarely the story of inevitable events, and it almost never appears that way as we're living through it. We don't see our own futures as inevitable, so why should we see the past that way? Instead, history is more often a story of unforeseen events and unforeseeable possibilities, of things that could have gone either way. Very little about the life of nations is certain, and even destiny is something quite different from inevitability. Every attempt to make history into a science has failed. The fact of our human freedom always gets in the way.

What we can say, though, is that there were landmark moments along the path of American history in which a civil war became much more likely. Chief among such moments was the Mexican War of 1846.

It is an event better remembered today by Mexicans (and Texans) than by most Americans. But the brief Mexican War had huge consequences for both countries, far out of proportion to its length. The war produced huge gains of territory for the United States. But those very gains had the effect of destroying the uneasy peace over slavery that the Missouri Compromise had established. They would lead to deeply unsettled circumstances that made an eventual conflict between North and South seem unavoidable. In more ways than one, the Mexican War provides support for the saying "be careful what you wish for."

Beginning in the 1820s, after Mexico had won its independence from Spain, it actively sought to attract immigrants from the American South who would settle and farm in its northern province of Texas. It more than got its wish, and got it more quickly than it could have imagined. Given the land hunger of so many westward-bound Americans, the vast and wide-open territory of the thinly settled Texas frontier was irresistible.

By 1825, Stephen F. Austin, son of a Missouri banker, had brought three hundred settlers into Texas and thereby contributed the first trickle of what would quickly swell to a flood of migrants. By 1830, newly arrived Americans outnumbered the Mexicans by three to one.

Such rapid changes made for conflict with existing residents, particularly given the sharp cultural differences between Protestant Americans and Catholic Mexicans. When the government of newly independent Mexico outlawed slavery in 1829 and insisted that the recent American immigrants convert to Roman Catholicism, both orders provoked intense resistance and open disobedience from the Americans. In 1830, Mexico tried to close itself off to further immigration, but the steady stream of incoming Americans continued.

Finally, matters came to a head with the rise to power in Mexico in 1834 of General Antonio López de Santa Anna. He was a haughty leader who had moved to strengthen central authority and make himself a virtual dictator. When Santa Anna abolished the Mexican Constitution of 1824 and dissolved the state legislatures, he provoked a rebellion in Texas and several other Mexican states. In the case of Texas, this soon turned into a struggle for Texas independence, in which the settlers were led by Sam Houston, a Virginia native who had served as a governor of Tennessee and was an adoptive member of the Cherokee tribe. The matter between Texas and Mexico would be settled by a clash of arms.

At first it went badly for the Texans. Santa Anna's army of six thousand moved swiftly against the resistance, obeying the command that all survivors be executed. After slaughtering a small but valiant American garrison holed up in the Alamo, an old Spanish mission in San Antonio that had been occupied by the rebels, the army proceeded to take the town of Goliad and to carry out a massacre of more than four hundred prisoners of war. Santa Anna seemed on the verge of a great and bloody victory.

But the fortunes would soon shift decisively. Less than a month later, at the Battle of the San Jacinto River, a largely untrained but fiercely motivated American force of volunteers, adventurers, and a few regulars under Houston's command would surprise the much larger Mexican army, defeat it in a matter of minutes, and take Santa Anna prisoner. The Texas Revolution was over and had been a resounding success. In October 1836, Houston would be elected president of a newly independent Republic of Texas.

A month later, a vote was held that indicated an overwhelming majority of Texans wanted their independent nation to become a part of the United States. Accordingly, Houston appealed to the U.S. government to consider such a move. But Andrew Jackson, then in the last months of his second term as U.S. president, hesitated to go that route. He feared that it would mean a war with Mexico and would inflame the slavery controversy, since the admission of Texas as a state, or as several states, would almost certainly come with pro-slavery strings attached. Jackson quickly extended diplomatic recognition to the new Republic of Texas but otherwise quietly deferred the question of Texas joining the United States, as did his successor, Martin van Buren. The matter drifted into the 1840s, unresolved.

In many ways, Jackson's and Van Buren's hesitation was prudent. The country did not need the unsettlement of a war with Mexico. But southerners in particular were not happy with the status quo in Texas, since it left Texas more and more vulnerable to falling under

British influence, and then serving Britain as an attractive alternative source of cotton and tariff-free markets – in other words, as a competitor.

Hesitation, too, was out of step with an increasingly self-confident national mood, which saw steady westward expansion as the realization of what the journalist John L. O'Sullivan, in advocating for Texas to become part of the United States, called "the fulfillment of our manifest destiny to overspread the continent allotted by Providence."

Today, when we hear the term *Manifest Destiny*, our reaction is likely to be negative. We may take it to be an expression of arrogance, a way of saying "step aside, we're taking over." And that reaction is not entirely wrong. But it reflects an incomplete understanding.

O'Sullivan himself, and the Young America movement of which he was a part, did not envision this "destiny" merely as a land acquisition project. His vision was far more idealistic than that. It was a vision that had sprung from the spirit of Jacksonian Democracy but that also recalled American dreams of previous generations, of America as a land of hope.

He said of his country that "we are the nation of progress, of individual freedom, of universal enfranchisement ... of the great experiment of liberty ... an Union of many Republics, comprising hundreds of happy millions, calling, owning no man master, but governed by God's natural and moral law of equality, the law of brotherhood." A country embracing the great North American landmass, stretching "from sea to shining sea," from the Atlantic to the Pacific Ocean: this was what the United States was meant to be, in the eyes of O'Sullivan and a great many others.

Small wonder that even a figure like the poet Walt Whitman embraced the continent-spanning vision of Manifest Destiny with unbounded enthusiasm. The desire to incorporate Texas was a part of it; so, too, was the rising "Oregon fever" that was luring caravans of westward-bound wagons across the continent along the Oregon Trail to explore the lush green possibilities of the Columbia and Willamette valleys. Yes, there were economic and political motives involved. Yes, there was arrogance, particularly when you consider the many Native American tribes inhabiting this vast territory. But there were also generous democratic ideals being put forward. Like so many things in history, Manifest Destiny was a mixed bag.

In the end, these forces proved too hard to resist. In 1844, Congress finally passed a joint resolution approving the annexation of Texas. As Andrew Jackson had anticipated, it led very soon to diplomatic trouble with Mexico. But the newly elected President James K. Polk, who took office in 1845, was determined to move ahead. Even as he was trying to settle the matter through negotiations, Polk had ordered General Zachary Taylor to take his army to Corpus Christi, on the northern side of the Rio Grande, in disputed territory. After an incident in which the Mexican army captured an American army patrol, killing or wounding sixteen men, Polk reacted by requesting, and receiving, congressional support for a war resolution on May 13, 1846.

Support for the war was overwhelming, but not unanimous. Some northerners, who feared that the war was meant merely to expand the number of slave states in the Union, opposed it strongly, with figures such as John Quincy Adams labeling it "a most unrighteous war." Daniel Webster, ever the defender of the national Union, feared that internal division might be the result. Yet the prospect of acquiring more land and the spirit of Manifest Destiny prevailed. Even some former opponents changed their position, reasoning that acquiring Mexican territory, which was considered too dry for cotton cultivation, might help the antislavery side.

As for the strictly military aspect of the war itself, it turned out to be highly successful, a sharp contrast to the near-disastrous War of 1812. General Taylor led his Rio Grande–based army into north central Mexico, taking the city of Monterrey and then defeating a superior force under Santa Anna at Buena Vista in February 1847. Soon after, General Winfield Scott landed a force farther south at the coastal city of Vera Cruz, and then marched west first to Puebla and then to Mexico City, entering the latter in triumph on September 13. A contingent of marines raised the American flag as they occupied the national palace, the legendary "halls of Montezuma."

With the signing of the Treaty of Guadalupe Hidalgo on February 2, 1848, Mexico abandoned its claims to Texas above the Rio Grande and ceded California and New Mexico to the United States. The result was an astounding transformation of the American map, almost like a second Louisiana Purchase. If the newly annexed land of Texas is included in the total, the United States had just acquired nearly 1 million square miles of additional territory. With the acquisition of the Oregon Territory two years before by treaty with Great Britain, the United States now had suddenly and dramatically achieved the dream of a transcontinental nation, including the acquisition of a new ocean coastline that featured the world-class harbors of San Francisco and San Diego.

It was like a sign from on high when, in early 1848, at the same time that General Scott's troops were occupying the Mexican capital and the Treaty of Guadalupe Hidalgo was being negotiated, gold was found at Sutter's Mill in California, some forty miles northeast of Sacramento. The resultant gold rush would bring three hundred thousand people to California in the next seven years, transforming it almost overnight from a remote Mexican frontier into a thriving American state.

Many Americans rejoiced at the American defeat of Mexico and saw it as an event of world-historical importance. It seemed to many that the country had "entered on a new epoch in its history," as a writer in *American Review* put it, an era that must "more than ever before, draw the world's history into the stream of ours." The discovery of gold in California seemed to be the crowning expression of divine favor. According to historian Robert W. Johannsen, "it was almost as if God had kept the gold hidden until the land came into the possession of the American republic." The way ahead seemed majestically clear and open.

But all this success and these giddy sentiments did not change the fact that the war had been controversial and that the amazing growth in the size and extent of the nation was soon going to prove a very deeply mixed blessing. As Jackson and other observers had predicted, the problem of slavery would reemerge, as decisions had to be made about whether to permit the extension of slavery into some, all, or none of the newly acquired lands. The delicately balanced Missouri Compromise that had been crafted in 1820 had calmed down the issue for the better part of three decades. But the compromise was a fragile and vulnerable thing, built on no defensible principles. It was more of a formula for delay than a genuine solution to a growing national problem. The rapid national growth of the 1840s could not help but challenge that settlement in a massive way.

Even before the war was over, there were already efforts to control its effects with regard to slavery. In 1846, Pennsylvania congressman David Wilmot, while endorsing the annexation of Texas as a

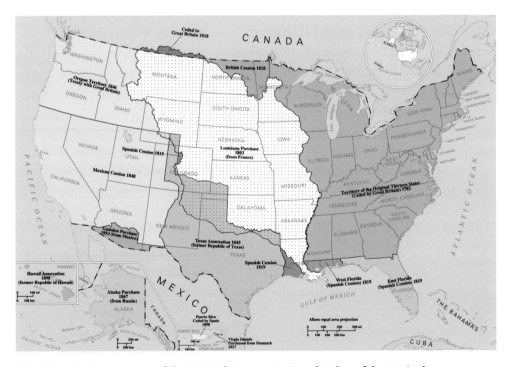

The historical expansion of the United States. National Atlas of the United States from the U.S. Department of the Interior.

slave state, proposed that the Congress forbid the introduction of slavery to any of the territories that might eventually be acquired in the Mexican War. His effort, dubbed the Wilmot Proviso, drew directly on the language and concepts of the Northwest Ordinance. It repeatedly passed the House, only to be rejected by the Senate; versions of the same idea were proposed again and again in the ensuing years.

Yet at the same time, Senator John C. Calhoun of South Carolina responded to the Wilmot Proviso's antislavery intentions with contempt. Slaveholders had a constitutional right, he insisted, to take their slaves into the territories if they wished. The prohibition being proposed, he argued, would violate the Fifth Amendment to the Constitution, which said that no one could be deprived of life or property – and slaves were considered legal property – without due process of law.

How to find a middle ground between two such positions, each claiming to draw upon fundamental sources? One way to manage the situation was to invoke the principle of "popular sovereignty," which was described by its chief proponent, Senator Lewis Cass of Michigan, as a system allowing the territories to "regulate their own internal concerns in their own way."

This is how it would work: instead of having a large national fight over the issue, popular sovereignty would allow for solutions to be arrived at separately, place by place, state by state, region by region, permitting the decision in each instance to be made by those who were closest to the situation and knew it best. It was an idea with much initial appeal to Americans, since it was in line with the fundamental idea of self-rule, of allowing the people to decide the laws by which they would be governed. But it ran directly against the natural-rights philosophy embedded in the Declaration of Independence, which declared that all men are created equal. Time would tell whether "popular sovereignty" could be effective in managing the nation's growing divisions.

In the meantime, however, events were forcing the issue. The California gold rush had created almost overnight a desperate need for a government that could bring law and order to a chaotic region. Something had to be done. General Taylor, who had been elected president in 1848 on the strength of his military achievements, suggested that California be admitted immediately as a free state, skipping entirely the territorial stage. The Californians themselves had already drawn up a constitution and created a state government that outlawed slavery.

Southerner planters were shocked by this turn of events. Taylor was himself a slaveholder, and many of them had supported him because they fully expected him to defend the introduction of slavery into the territories. They felt betrayed. And the stakes were very high, since the admission of California as a free state would upset the balance between slave and free states in the Senate and leave the South a minority. The Congress found itself in an uproar, and there began to be serious talk of southern secession.

Into this condition of high drama strode Henry Clay of Kentucky, the great deal maker of the Senate, now in his seventies and in failing health. He took charge of the situation and fashioned a complex package of eight different resolutions that would, he hoped, settle "all questions in controversy between the free and slave States."

A great debate ensued, one of the greatest in the Senate's storied history, featuring lengthy and memorable speeches by Clay, Calhoun, Webster, William Seward, and a host of others. Clay and Webster favored compromise, while the pro-slavery Calhoun and the antislavery Seward opposed it. But thanks to the skillful political work of Stephen A. Douglas of Illinois, among others, the measures making up what would become known as the Compromise of 1850 were passed.

Chief among these measures were the admission of California as a free state, the use of popular sovereignty to decide the slavery status of the other territories arising out of the Mexican War, and the passing of a much-strengthened Fugitive Slave Law, which would require residents of the free states to cooperate in the capture and return of escaped slaves to their owners. The last of these was to be the South's compensation for the unequal standing that the admission of California imposed upon it. The South would accept the permanent minority status it feared, on condition that the North agreed to protect, in an active way, the "peculiar institution" that had come to be deemed essential to the southern way of life.

It was a sweeping effort, the last to be undertaken by the great generation of Clay, Calhoun, and Webster, to address the growing national crisis and secure the Union. Within two years, all three men would be dead. But the nation breathed a giant sigh of relief, as its politicians had moved back from the brink, and an outburst of patriotic harmony took hold for a time. "Let us cease agitating, stop the debate, and drop the subject," said Douglas, representing the next generation in the Senate. For a time, the overwhelming majority of Americans seemed inclined to agree. But not for long.

In retrospect, it is hard to see how anyone could have believed

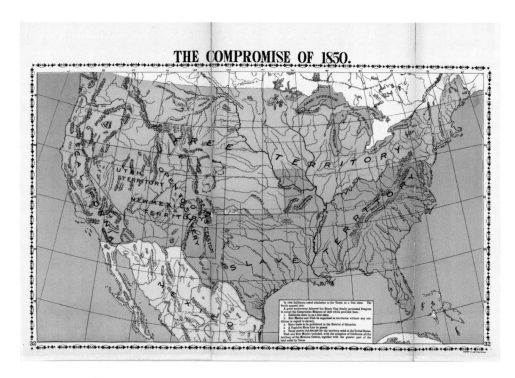

The territorial consequences of the Compromise of 1850, from a 1911 atlas in the Geography and Map Division of the Library of Congress.

that this compromise could hold. But as we said at the outset of this chapter, we should make the effort to try to see the past as its actors saw it and understand the depth of their dilemma. More than ever, the country still had the wolf by the ear. The great gains of the Mexican War had only increased the size and ferocity of that wolf.

The Compromise of 1850 did not provide any ultimate solutions. It did buy time for the Union's future. It reduced political tension, quieted secession talk, and allowed breathing room for the emergence of other, better solutions. It would allow the country to turn its attention back to its real business, the settling of a giant continent. Often in politics, problems are not solved so much as they are managed; and it is sometimes in the unromantic work of preventing the worst from happening that statesmanship shows itself to best effect.

On the other hand, a festering wound does not heal itself. The endless postponement of questions of principle may lead to a far worse reckoning when that reckoning comes. Moral reformers are sometimes said to be guilty of "crackpot idealism," which is fair enough; sometimes they are unrealistic and blind in their demands. But there is also such a thing as "crackpot realism," a mistaken belief that the endless deferral of ideals is a more "realistic" political strategy than the effort, however difficult, to take hold of the problem, and realize those ideals.

It may be an especially hard strategy to follow in a land of hope. "What happens to a dream deferred?" asked the African American poet Langston Hughes, years later. "Does it dry up / like a raisin in the sun? / Or fester like a sore – / and then run? ... Or does it explode?" An answer was coming soon.

20 · THE EMERGENCE OF LINCOLN

IT SOON BECAME CLEAR that a strict fugitive slave law was simply not going to be acceptable to many northerners. The reason is not hard to find. It was one thing for northerners to accept the existence of slavery "down there," where they did not have to confront it in their daily lives. But the Fugitive Slave Law was something quite different. It required northerners to support the peculiar institution directly. It required them to be actively engaged in cooperating with the tracking down, capture, and sending back of escapees who were merely seeking the conditions under which they could enjoy the life, liberty, and pursuit of happiness to which they were naturally entitled.

Under these circumstances, toleration felt the same as participation. Such a law was doomed to generate intense resistance, and ultimately to be ineffective. The Wisconsin Supreme Court declared it unconstitutional, Vermont passed laws effectively nullifying it and assisting captured slaves, and Ralph Waldo Emerson denounced it as a "filthy enactment" that should be broken "on the earliest occasion." Abolitionist pastor Luther Lee of Syracuse, New York, declared simply, "The Fugitive Slave Law is a war upon God, upon his law, and upon the rights of humanity.... To obey it, or to aid in its enforcement, is treason against God and humanity, and involves a guilt equal to the guilt of violating every one of the ten commandments." Given such feelings, the appearance in 1852 of Stowe's

Uncle Tom's Cabin could not have been more timely, as a glimpse into the harsh realities of slave life and the perils faced by freedom-seeking slaves.

Meanwhile, another threat to the uneasy settlement of 1850 was brewing, in a different quarter: the effort to create a transcontinental railroad that would link the two coasts. That such a rail line should be built was beyond question. But *where* to build it – that was another question altogether, and powerful economic interests would be at stake in the decision. In the end, there were two main rival proposals: a southern one, promoted by Jefferson Davis of Mississippi, and a north central one, promoted by Stephen A. Douglas of Illinois.

Douglas was a deal-making politician. To make his proposal more acceptable to southerners, Douglas proposed that the land west of Missouri be organized into two territories, the Kansas Territory and the Nebraska Territory, with each being allowed to settle by popular sovereignty the question of whether slavery would be permitted.

This was a far more momentous proposal than it might seem. Since both proposed territories were north of the 36°30′ line established by the Missouri Compromise, Douglas's bill was opening up the possibility of introducing slavery into territory where it had previously been forbidden. He was, in effect, proposing to repeal the Missouri Compromise, the principal instrument that had kept a lid on the sectional conflict for three decades. The proposal led to three months of bitter debate, but in the end, both houses of Congress passed the Kansas–Nebraska Act of 1854, and President Franklin Pierce signed it into law. It was a reckless blunder.

Douglas had assumed that the homesteaders moving into the Kansas Territory from the Midwest would vote to exclude slavery. But what if the migrants brought their slaves with them? What if they sought to game the eventual vote and flip Kansas into a slave state? Such were the practical and moral failings of popular sovereignty. Soon violent conflicts developed between the competing settlement communities, with a pro-slavery mob's attack on the town of Lawrence being answered by an even more vicious attack by the abolitionist John Brown and his sons, who hacked to death, in front of their screaming families, five men from a pro-slavery farm near Pottawatomie Creek.

The spectacle of "Bleeding Kansas" became a national disgrace, as the embattled would-be state soon found itself pulled between the claims of two competing governments and two rival constitutions. So much for popular sovereignty as a way to tamp down conflict!

Nor was the violence confined to Kansas in its effects. On May 20, 1856, Senator Charles Sumner of Massachusetts delivered an angry speech denouncing the Kansas–Nebraska Act on the floor of the U.S. Senate, decrying it as an instrument of "the Slave Power," with the aim of producing "a new Slave State, hideous offspring of such a crime." Sumner also went after specific individuals in a very personal way, including Senator Andrew Butler of South Carolina, whom he accused of having embraced "the harlot, slavery" as his "mistress," a loaded insult that seemed almost calculated to generate a fierce rejoinder. The response came two days later, when Butler's cousin, Congressman Preston Brooks, confronted Sumner at his desk in the Senate chamber after an adjournment, denounced the speech as "a libel on South Carolina and Mr. Butler," and proceeded to beat him over the head with a heavy gold-headed cane, nearly killing him.

The reaction to this incident was also telling. In the North, there were rallies in support of Sumner in Boston and a half-dozen other cities, and Emerson's comments were representative: "I do not see how a barbarous community and a civilized community can constitute one state. I think we must get rid of slavery, or we must get rid of freedom."

But the Southern view was different. The *Richmond Enquirer* praised the attack and asserted that Sumner should be caned "every morning." Brooks received hundreds of new canes in endorsement of his assault, and one of them was inscribed "Hit him again."

The territorial consequences of the Kansas–Nebraska Act, from a 1911 atlas in the Geography and Map Division of the Library of Congress.

By the time he delivered his fateful speech, Sumner had become a member of a new political party, the Republican Party. It had arisen in direct response to the Kansas–Nebraska Act. Drawing its membership from antislavery elements in the Democratic, Whig, and Free Soil Parties, the new party had unified around the issue of opposing the extension of slavery into the territories. By 1856, it was the second largest party in the country. The largest, the Democratic Party, was struggling to avoid a splintering between its northern and southern elements, just as the Whig Party had already done before it. The Republican Party was from its start almost entirely a party of the North.

As the sole remaining national party, then, the Democrats expected to do well in the presidential campaign of 1856 with their highly experienced candidate, James Buchanan of Pennsylvania, who had served in both houses of Congress, as an ambassador to

Russia and Great Britain, and as Polk's secretary of state. The Republicans campaigned on a platform that combined classic Whig issues, such as internal improvements (including a transcontinental railroad) and protective tariffs, with firm opposition to the expansion of slavery into the territories. It condemned the Kansas–Nebraska Act and its disregard for the Missouri Compromise and condemned slavery as a "relic of barbarism." It was the first time a national party had declared its opposition to slavery.

Buchanan, however, was a familiar face, elected to maintain the status quo in a turbulent time, and he believed that meant making conciliatory gestures and concessions toward the South: on states' rights, on territorial expansion, on popular sovereignty, and on slavery. Yet before Buchanan could even get started, something momentous came along to widen and deepen the chasm between the sections. A mere two days after his inauguration in March 1857, the Supreme Court handed down its decision in the long-awaited case of *Dred Scott v. Sandford*. And it was a blockbuster decision, one that would greatly add to the tensions between the sections.

The case was a bit complicated. Dred Scott had been born a slave in Virginia. He had been sold to an army surgeon named Dr. John Emerson, who took him to Illinois, a free state, and to the Wisconsin Territory, also free, where Scott married and had two daughters. After his master's death, in 1846, Scott sued in the Missouri courts for his freedom, on the grounds that his residence in a free state and free territory had made him free. The case wended its way through the courts and finally was appealed to the Supreme Court, which was then presided over by Roger B. Taney, a Democrat from the border south state of Maryland.

The court ruled against Scott. Taney, who wrote the majority opinion, was not content to decide the case narrowly. He wanted to resolve the issue of slavery in the territories once and for all. Far from doing so, his Court's decision blew up what little remaining national agreement there was.

There were three main thrusts of Taney's opinion.

First, he dismissed Scott's claims, arguing that Scott did not even have legal standing to sue because he was not a citizen; and he was not a citizen because the Framers of the Constitution did not intend to extend citizenship rights to blacks.

Second, he argued (distinctly echoing Calhoun) that Congress lacked the power to deprive any person of his property without due process of law, and because slaves were property, slavery could not be excluded from any federal territory or state.

Third and finally, he ruled that the Missouri Compromise was not merely rendered moot by the Kansas–Nebraska Act; it was *unconstitutional*, and had been all along, because it had invalidly excluded slavery from Wisconsin and other northern territories.

The decision appeared to doom the doctrine of popular sovereignty, since it would seem that, if the federal government could not exclude slavery from the territories, neither could a territorial government. With the Missouri Compromise in tatters, everything it had decided was now up for reconsideration – even overturning.

Some radical southerners, encouraged by the decision, called for the establishment of a federal slave code to protect their property in human flesh. These radicals felt events were turning their way. They sensed, with reason, that President Buchanan was on their side, perhaps even had known in advance of, and encouraged, the *Dred Scott* decision, and had hoped it would settle the slavery question once and for all.

Northerners had similar suspicions of Buchanan: that he was a conscious tool of the southern pro-slavery conspiracy. His presidency was not going to be the instrument that would lead the nation out of its state of division. When a financial panic hit the country in 1857, with disproportionate effects upon the North, it seemed further confirmation of that fact. Leadership would have to come from elsewhere.

All eyes now turned to Stephen Douglas, the "Little Giant" of Illinois, the last remaining prominent Democrat who had national and not merely sectional sources of support, and whose campaign for reelection to the Senate in 1858 was likely to be a warm-up for his long-desired run for the presidency in 1860. If anyone could hold the Democratic Party, and thereby the country, together, it was he.

But he would face a formidable challenge for that Illinois Senate seat from Abraham Lincoln, a rising star in the Republican Party. Lincoln had been a successful trial lawyer and one-term Whig Congressman and had left politics for a time, but had been goaded back into the fray by his fierce opposition to the Kansas–Nebraska Act. Lincoln had opposed Douglas from the very beginning of the controversy over that act, and he was the natural person to run against him and his ideas.

Lincoln's life story would become the stuff of American legend. He was the uncommon common man born to humble frontier circumstances who rose in the world by dint of his sheer determination and effort. Born in Kentucky in 1809, his early life, he once said, could be summarized in one sentence: "the short and simple annals of the poor." We don't know much about his early life. We know that he moved from Kentucky to Indiana to Illinois, a typical pioneer farm boy, burdened with the tasks of hauling water, chopping wood, plowing, harvesting. We know that he hated farm work so much that he would seize the opportunity to do almost anything else. We know that he had almost no formal schooling yet was a voracious reader, with a great love of words and of oratory.

When young man Lincoln arrived in New Salem, Illinois, as, by his own description, "a piece of floating driftwood," he was a nobody. But he soon found employment as a clerk, introduced himself into the life of the community, became popular, was appointed postmaster, and ran for and on the second try was elected to the Illinois General Assembly. As Lincoln said in announcing his candidacy for the General Assembly in 1832, he "was born, and [had] ever remained, in the most humble walks of life," without "wealthy or popular relations or friends to recommend" him. But he had been given unprecedented opportunity to realize his potential by the right set of conditions.

For Lincoln, his success was a fulfillment of the spirit of the

Declaration of Independence, which Lincoln revered and repeatedly returned to. Its affirmation of the equal worth of all people, and their equal entitlement to life, liberty, and the pursuit of happiness, was a lifelong touchstone for him. For him, that equality meant the equal right of all people to the fruits of their own labors, a principle grounded not in the will of governments or men but in the dictates of Nature and Nature's God. It was no surprise that Lincoln loathed slavery from his earliest youth, believing it to be a form of theft that allowed one class of men to steal from another class.

So this son of the frontier seemed to have found his moment in the territorial controversy of the 1850s and in the newly founded Republican Party. His Senate candidacy gave him a moral platform to oppose Douglas's politically skillful but unprincipled cunning, and particularly to oppose the abandonment of high principles that came along with the doctrine of popular sovereignty. In July 1858, he challenged Douglas to a series of seven public debates, and Douglas accepted the challenge.

The debates became classics of their kind. They were political debates, with all the verbal trickery, aggressiveness, and crafty trap setting such debates generally involve. Lincoln tried to make Douglas look like a radical pro-slavery, pro–*Dred Scott* southern sympathizer, something he wasn't. Douglas tried to make Lincoln look like a dangerous abolitionist, something he wasn't either.

But they also engaged the questions besetting the nation in a rational and surprisingly complex way, one that dignified and elevated the process of democratic deliberation. We would do well to recover their example. Our own era's content-free presidential "debates" are hardly even a pale imitation.

Lincoln went on to lose the Illinois Senate election to Douglas. But the strength of his arguments endured, and made the election a close one. His strong showing in the Illinois Senate campaign had brought him to the attention of the whole nation and made him a plausible Republican candidate for president in 1860.

And there were other suggestive political takeaways from 1858. All across the North, the Republicans made significant gains in the congressional elections, a development that raised the concerns of southerners, not only because of the party's antislavery commitments, but also because of its economic program and its support for high tariffs. The Republican Party fell only four seats short of an absolute majority. An ascendant sectional Republican Party and a disintegrating national Democratic Party: these developments suggested trouble ahead for the Union itself.

Another, and perhaps the last, fire bell in the night came with abolitionist John Brown's audacious raid on the federal arsenal at Harpers Ferry, Virginia, on the night of October 16, 1859. Brown's hatred of slavery had only hardened and intensified in the years since his Pottawatomie Massacre. He was more convinced than ever that it was God's will for him to strike a powerful blow against the empire of slavery.

His plan was to seize guns from the arsenal and use them to arm the slaves of the region, and fuel a slave uprising, which could lead to the creation of a slave-run state. His efforts failed, with the loss of fourteen lives, including two of his sons. Brown would be captured and hanged on December 2, but not before delivering a memorable speech in which he offered his life "for the furtherance of the ends of justice."

As with Preston Brooks, so with John Brown, the response to his actions and his execution was profoundly divided. Southerners were horrified. They took his violent rampage to be an indication of what the North had in store for them. Northerners like Emerson, however, saw Brown as a martyr and saint, who "make[s] the gallows as glorious as the cross." Unfortunately, matters had come to a point where the extremists on both sides reinforced one another's perspective. There was not much room for moderates who saw slavery as neither an absolute good or an unmitigated evil but a problem that might eventually be solved by peaceful means.

By the time the presidential election of 1860 was approaching, the Democratic Party was finally splitting apart. Douglas was the likely nominee of the party's national convention, but he was unacceptable to southerners and Buchanan supporters. They left the party convention and nominated their own candidate, Vice President John Breckenridge of Kentucky. Douglas would be nominated by the remaining delegates on a platform of popular sovereignty and enforcement of the Fugitive Slave Law. But the Breckenridge Democrats would produce an extreme platform calling for no restrictions on slavery in the territories and the annexation of slavery-rich Cuba. Other dissidents would form a new party, the Constitutional Union Party, which nominated John Bell of Tennessee and sought, through a deliberately vague platform, to encourage the moderation of passions and the enforcement of existing laws.

The Republicans nominated Lincoln, choosing him over the somewhat more radical William H. Seward, as an effort to win over waverers. The divisions among the Democrats made the prospect of a Republican victory very likely – but also very challenging. For one thing, not one of the four candidates was capable of being a truly national candidate or mounting an effective national campaign.

The election returns for November 1860 bore this out. Lincoln won 180 electoral votes from all eighteen free states – and from *only* those states. He got not a single electoral vote from the South. Douglas, the only candidate who might have been able to appeal to the nation as a whole, despite an energetic campaign that took him down into the hostile Deep South states in a desperate quest for support, received a pathetic twelve electoral votes, finishing a far-distant last in the four-way race.

Lincoln's election was momentous in a great many ways. But first and foremost, he was the first president elected to office on the basis of an entirely regional victory. Some southerners had warned in advance of the election that such an outcome could mean that the South had no choice but secession from the Union.

Could a state decide to leave the Union after all this time? The "compact" theory of the Constitution, which had long been favored by many southerners, seemed to offer a constitutional basis for doing so. In this view, because the Constitution was a "compact" between states, those states had a right to withdraw from the compact, just as any contract can be revoked or terminated if a party

can state sufficient cause for doing so. In addition, many southerners strongly believed that any act of secession would be squarely in
the tradition of the American Revolution, which had been justified
on the grounds that the people have the right to overthrow or
replace any government that fails to reflect the consent of the
governed.

Soon after the election, South Carolina did just that, repealing its
1788 ratification of the Constitution and dissolving its union with
the other states, and citing the election of Lincoln as justification.
By February 1, 1861, six other southern states (Mississippi, Florida,
Texas, Georgia, Louisiana, and Alabama) had followed suit and by
February 7 had formed themselves into the Confederate States of
America, adopting a Constitution that was virtually identical to the
U.S. Constitution, but with added limits on the government's power
to impose tariffs or restrict slavery. It elected Jefferson Davis of
Mississippi as president and Alexander Stephens of Georgia as vice
president.

Even this impressive show of organization and strength would
not have been effective if there had been sufficient pushback from
national leaders. For one thing, the immensely important state of
Virginia, along with the other Upper South states, had not yet committed to secession. It was possible that those states could be kept
from joining the others. Yet James Buchanan, in the four months
of his lame-duck presidency, did nothing. He believed that resistance would only increase the South's sense of grievance and hoped
that the many ongoing efforts at reconciliation might succeed in
bringing the country back from the brink.

As a last, desperate move, the Congress narrowly passed a constitutional amendment, which came to be called the Corwin Amendment, supported by Lincoln, Seward, and other Republicans, that
would have protected slavery where it already existed.

That deeply committed antislavery men like Lincoln and Seward
were desperate enough to support a measure so contrary to their
own moral sentiments – a measure as permanent as a constitutional amendment! – speaks volumes about the feeling of immense

and immediate peril that had suddenly enveloped the land and the terrifying abyss that seemed to be opening up before its leaders.

The amendment passed the House easily and passed the Senate by one vote above the required two-thirds majority, on March 2, 1861, two days before Lincoln's inauguration. Had it gone on to be ratified by the states, it would have been the Thirteenth Amendment. But it was destined never to be ratified.

Instead, there would be secession and then four years of appalling war: a war to preserve the Union, but one that also would transform it in the process. Adoption of the Corwin Amendment might have bought some time, at best – just as the Missouri Compromise had. But it would have done so at terrible cost. It would have made permanent the deepest moral wound in the nation's life, written it clearly into the Constitution – something that the Framers deliberately refused to do. It would have rendered the cultural gulf between North and South permanently impassable. It would have made the ultimate reckoning even more horrific. It was not the solution that the nation needed.

In fact, matters had come to the point where it was no solution at all. Lincoln himself had predicted, in his "House Divided" speech of June 16, 1858, that the nation could not endure "permanently half slave and half free," but that it would have to "become all one thing or all the other." Events were in the process of proving that prediction to be correct.

21 · THE HOUSE DIVIDES

PRESIDENT-ELECT ABRAHAM LINCOLN moved cautiously during the four months between his election and his taking office. He had to, because he would face extraordinarily weighty decisions from the moment he became president.

Here are some of the questions he had to consider: How active should he be in trying to prevent secession? How generous should he be toward the Southern states? How could he persuade the states of the Upper South not to follow the Deep South states into secession? And if secession occurred anyway, what should he do about it? Should he go to war and oppose secession by use of military force? Or should he allow the Southern states to go in peace? If he did the former, how does one go about fighting a war to force the nation to stay together? Was such a thing even possible? Or, if he let the South go, might that leave the United States so weakened that its rising status in the world would soon end – and then be reversed?

As Lincoln assembled his cabinet, he pondered all these things and more. Yet he gave few outward signs of what he was planning to do. Much of the public was very nervous about what to expect from this lanky, awkward man of the prairies who had no experience as an executive leader.

His thinking began to emerge more clearly in his inaugural address on March 4, 1861. It tried to strike a peacemaking tone. The South, he insisted, had nothing to fear from him. He would protect slavery where it already existed. He was willing to accept the Corwin Amendment, which had been passed by both houses of

Congress and would have incorporated the protection of slavery into the Constitution. He would enforce the Fugitive Slave Act, so long as free blacks were protected against its misuse. He promised not to use force against the South, unless the South took up arms in rebellion.

But secession was another matter. Lincoln was crystal clear about that: he would not tolerate it. The Union, he asserted firmly, was perpetual and unbreakable. Seceding from it was impossible. What South Carolina and the other Deep South states were doing was wrong.

So there was a vein of iron in the speech. But Lincoln concluded not with a threat but with an emotional appeal to unity, and to the shared memories that had held the United States together for its eight and a half decades as a nation. "We are not enemies, but friends," he pleaded. "We must not be enemies." The passions of the moment "must not break our bonds of affection." He concluded the speech with an unforgettable image of hope and an appeal to the shared past. "The mystic chords of memory," he said, "stretching from every battlefield and patriot grave to every living heart and hearthstone all over this broad land, will yet swell the chorus of the Union, when again touched, as surely they will be, by the better angels of our nature."

"The mystic chords of memory" – that was one of the finest phrases ever spoken in a presidential speech. Such soaring presidential oratory had not been heard in Washington since the days of Thomas Jefferson. But it was to no avail, since it did not sway the hearts and minds of the Southern leaders. Lincoln's strategy would soon be forced to shift, though, when he was faced with his first crisis: the siege of Fort Sumter, a federal facility located on a small island in the harbor of Charleston, South Carolina. Secessionists in South Carolina had demanded that the fort be evacuated, something Buchanan had refused to do; but Buchanan's effort to resupply the isolated post had been driven away by Confederate artillery fire.

That was the situation when Lincoln became president. When Sumter's commanding officer, Major Robert Anderson, declared that he and his sixty-nine men had only a few weeks' supplies left, Lincoln made the decision to attempt again to resupply him and the fort. Unwilling to permit this, the Confederates opened fire on the fort and, after more than thirty hours of bombardment, forced its surrender in advance of the arrival of the resupply effort.

This seemed to be a defeat for the Union. But actually it was a triumph. Lincoln had shrewdly maneuvered the South Carolinians into firing the first shots. If war was unavoidable, he reasoned, then it should begin on terms favorable to the Union. He could easily have chosen other, more aggressive measures. For example, he could have wasted no time in attacking the South Carolinian forces head-on.

But any such measures would have sacrificed the moral high ground, always important in modern warfare, and especially important in the conduct of a civil war whose success would depend upon favorable public opinion. It was of great value for Lincoln, and the federal cause, to be able to claim in truthfulness that they were not the aggressors and that their response was in self-defense.

Immediately after the surrender of Fort Sumter, which produced an outburst of anger in the North, Lincoln called on the Northern states to supply seventy-five thousand militiamen to help in the battle against the Confederacy. That effort would be followed by a blockade of Southern ports. These actions were enough to bring four Upper South states into the Confederacy, including the all-important Virginia, as well as Tennessee, Arkansas, and North Carolina. However, the border states of Kentucky, Missouri, Delaware, and Maryland still did not join. It would be an important objective of Lincoln's, throughout the war to keep the border states in the Union and out of the Confederacy.

And so the war began. Neither side expected anything like the lengthy and destructive struggle that was to come. Even so, vital principles were in conflict, and the conflicts extended back many years. Southerners believed that Lincoln and the North were violating the important principle of self-determination by refusing to allow the Southern states to do as a majority of their citizens wanted. Lincoln, on the other hand, saw secession as a form of anarchy, an action that, by refusing to accept the results of a legitimate election, would discredit the very idea of democracy itself around the world.

For Lincoln, the preservation of the Union was the chief goal of the war. All other objectives were less important to him. It is important to stress this. It was not until well into the war that the overthrow of slavery became an important part of the Northern agenda.

Going into the war, the North enjoyed huge advantages. It had the larger population (22 million to 9 million, with the latter number including 4 million slaves), held more states (twenty-three to eleven), had a larger economy, had control of the nation's banking and financial system, contained most of the nation's industry and most of its iron and coal, and boasted huge advantages in transportation (more wagons, ships, and horses and 70 percent of the nation's railroads) and a decent-sized navy, and on and on. Totaling up the relative assets of the two sides, the South didn't seem to have had a prayer of success.

But wars are not won merely by making lists of assets. Such lists would not reflect some very real advantages that the Confederacy brought to the struggle. First and foremost was the fact that its war objectives were simple and easily met. The two sides needed to achieve very different things. To attain their objective of political independence, the Confederate states needed only to hang on to the territory they claimed for themselves, territory they already controlled. In other words, they had only to fight a defensive war on familiar and friendly territory to win.

Meanwhile, the North would have to conquer and occupy an area the size of Mexico – and then convince it to rejoin the nation it had just angrily left. The Confederates would be defending their homeland. But the North was fighting for an abstract idea, "the Union." In addition, many of the nation's most talented military leaders, men such as Robert E. Lee, Joseph E. Johnston, and Thomas J. "Stonewall" Jackson, were Southerners who had left the U.S. Army to join the Confederate cause. With such leaders, with such clear objectives, and with the legendary marksmanship and fighting spirit of Southern soldiers, the rebel force might be able to put up a compelling resistance.

The South had other reasons for optimism, which did not seem unrealistic at the war's outset. It seemed entirely possible, for example, that European demand for Southern cotton might eventually cause one or another country to extend support to the Confederacy. In addition, it was reasonable to believe that the people of the North might tire of an extended war, particularly one to reimpose a Union upon people who no longer wanted it. In that sense, time was on the South's side.

Lincoln faced a very complicated job, then, as a minority president whose support was neither deep nor wide. The successful conduct of the kind of war he was facing would depend on a large measure of patience. Without a steady stream of clear victories in the field of battle, the Northern public might well become restless, lose patience with the war effort, and force Lincoln into making a negotiated settlement.

In addition, the Union didn't start out with a true national army. When Lincoln issued his call-up to the state militias in the wake of Fort Sumter, what rolled into Washington was a motley assortment of men whose irregular uniforms reflected the natural diversity of what was still a very loosely organized republic. Some states dressed their fighting men in blue; others were in combinations of gray, emerald, black, or red. The New Yorkers sported baggy red breeches, purple Oriental blouses, and red fezzes. One observer said that the first Union forces assembling in Washington looked less like a serious army than "like a circus on parade." This was not a condition that would last, but it was indicative of the obstacles that both Lincoln and his military leaders would face, at the beginning, in welding together a capable fighting unit. It would take time.

The illusion that the war could be ended quickly, however, was widespread. Lincoln had signed up the first volunteers for enlistments of only ninety days. He hoped that a single effective stroke could end the South's ability to resist and allow the Union army to march straight to the Confederate capital at Richmond and put an end to the war. That hope would be shattered on July 21 by the first major land encounter of the war, the First Battle of Bull Run just south of Washington. Confederate general Jackson humiliated a force of thirty-seven thousand raw Union troops, sending them racing back to Washington in a panic, along with a contingent of curiosity seekers and observers. There would not be a single decisive stroke by the Union forces.

In the meantime, General-in-Chief Winfield Scott, who had been a hero in the War of 1812 and the Mexican War, but was now seventy-four years old and in poor health, was developing the overall Union strategy. His approach became known as the Anaconda Plan, named for the large tropical snake that defeats its prey by squeezing it to death. The Union would use the superiority of the U.S. Navy to blockade the Southern ports, which would have punishing effects upon the import-dependent Southern economy. In addition, the Union would take possession of New Orleans and the Mississippi River, which would allow it to control vital commerce on the river and to split the Confederacy in two.

It was a good strategy. Had it been followed persistently, it could conceivably have led to a rapid and relatively bloodless outcome to the war. But it had one major defect: it took too long to have any visible effect. This was not a military defect, but it was a political one. Lincoln recognized that fact when he replaced Scott with General George B. McClellan, who confidently promised to push the war forward.

The snobbish and fussy McClellan soon proved to be unsatisfactory to Lincoln, however. A stiffly professional West Point graduate who believed in thorough preparation, McClellan insisted on putting his troops through extensive training before going into battle, not moving on Virginia until March 1862. Lincoln's impatient complaints were brushed aside by the arrogant general, who made no secret of his scorn for the president's intelligence.

Finally, McClellan devised an ingenious strategy for attacking

the Confederate capital. Instead of attempting to advance southward over the difficult terrain of northern Virginia, he moved an
army of 121,500 men down the Potomac River and the Chesapeake
Bay to the neck of land between the James and York Rivers, the
peninsula containing Jamestown and Yorktown. They would come
into Richmond from the southeast, by the back door.

This opening move in McClellan's Peninsula Campaign worked
well and put his army within twenty-five miles of the Confederate
capital. But then, in what became a pattern with him, McClellan
hesitated and frittered away the advantage of his initial success.
Through a series of tactically brilliant Confederate moves, many of
them led by Robert E. Lee, McClellan's advance would be repulsed,
and he was eventually forced to retreat.

Lee, buoyed by these triumphs and intent on an even greater
success, decided on a bold move of invading the North, specifically
the enemy territory of Maryland and Pennsylvania. It would be risky.
But Lee was willing to take the risk, considering the benefit that
would come to the Confederate cause, especially in the eyes of potential European supporters, from a victory on the enemy's own turf.

It turned out to be even riskier than Lee could have guessed. He
did not know that McClellan had obtained a copy of his secret orders,
detailing his battle plan for the next engagement with Union troops.
McClellan thus had a huge advantage. But he again failed to press
it and gave Lee time to gather his forces. The two armies clashed at
Antietam Creek in Maryland on September 17, 1862. It was the
bloodiest single day of the entire war, with some 22,000 men
killed or wounded.

The immediate result of the battle at Antietam appeared inconclusive. For all intents and purposes, it was a standoff, despite the
North's prior knowledge of Confederate plans and its possession of a
two-to-one advantage in troop numbers going into the battle. True,
the progress of Lee's army was stopped cold; his northern-invasion
ideas had been thwarted so far. But McClellan had failed to exploit
this fact, something he easily could have done. He could have turned
a standoff into a smashing victory simply by bringing in additional

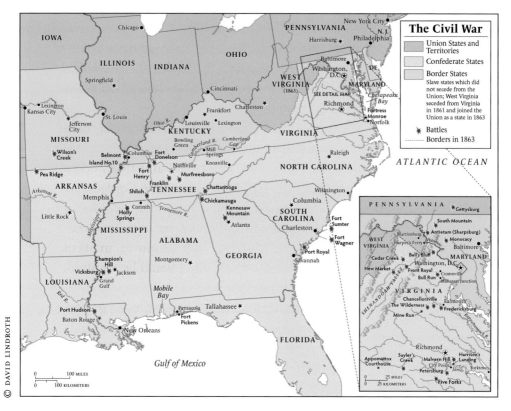

Major campaigns of the Civil War.

troops that were being held in reserve, and continuing to bring the fight to Lee, pushing him back to the Potomac River behind him and trapping him.

All he had to do was seize the moment. But he didn't, and thanks to his indecision, the remnants of Lee's army were able to slip away and lived to fight another day. Lincoln was furious. He had expected far better results from such favorable circumstances. He removed McClellan from command, replacing him with the more aggressive General Ambrose Burnside.

Yet, for all its disappointing aspects, that bloody standoff at Antietam Creek turned out to be an important *strategic victory* for the Union. For one thing, it had denied the South a victory it had needed very badly. Even more importantly, Antietam had given the North a great opportunity, precisely the opportunity that it had failed to produce for the South: the right moment to make an appeal for the favorable attention of the world.

Even before Antietam, Lincoln had already been thinking about ways he could weaken the institution of slavery. Even though he had not been an abolitionist in his earlier politics, he had always been outspoken regarding slavery as "an unqualified evil" whose eventual elimination was an ultimate end for which he fervently wished. He was getting pressure from Republican and abolitionist groups to act. He knew that such a move on the part of his government would gain the Union cause much favor and support in foreign capitals and counteract any strictly economic appeal of the Southern cause. Several concerns had been holding him back, though. Some were constitutional, some were military, and some were social or political. Some were questions of high principle, whereas others were questions of practical politics.

In the first category was the fact that slavery was protected under the Constitution, a fact that he himself had repeatedly stressed and even campaigned on. Lincoln had an unusually high regard for the law in general and a near-religious reverence for the Constitution in particular. He believed that the strength of the Union depended on the nation's unflagging devotion to that document. If he were ever going to use his executive authority to restrict or end slavery, it would have to be done in a completely constitutional way.

There were several other concerns on his mind. As mentioned before, he needed to keep the support of border states, such as his native Kentucky and Missouri, both of which were slave states but had not joined the Confederacy. A sudden move toward abolition might tip those states to the other side. Furthermore, it was not even clear that most Northerners would accept abolition. Lincoln was a canny politician, careful not to get too far out in front of public opinion.

Nevertheless, by July 1862, he was convinced that the time had come for the national government to adopt a strongly antislavery position. He believed that such a position could be justified both on military grounds (the freed slaves could fight in the war effort) and diplomatic ones (to attract support from Europe). He would have preferred to see slavery abolished by the individual states through their own laws, with compensation for slave owners and federal aid for freedmen who wished to emigrate. But he had not enjoyed any success in persuading the border states to consider that approach and was now prepared to use the powers of his own office.

He had discussed the possibility of an emancipation proclamation with his cabinet and received a decidedly mixed response from them. Several feared anarchy in the South and possible foreign intervention. His secretary of state, William Seward, favored the idea but advised him to wait to issue the proclamation until there had been a significant Union victory.

That was exactly what Lincoln did. On September 22, 1862, just five days after Antietam, he made public the first part of the Emancipation Proclamation, a preliminary statement that outlined the intent of the whole Proclamation, announcing that all slaves in the states at war with the United States as of January 1, 1863, would be "then, thenceforward, and forever free." The second part of the Proclamation would be issued on that later date. Theoretically, Confederate states that ceased their rebellion by that date would have been allowed to keep their slaves.

That last item underscores something important about the Emancipation Proclamation: it was designed as a war measure. Lincoln handled the matter this way out of his profound respect for the Constitution. He insisted that during peacetime, he had no power to abolish slavery where it already existed and enjoyed constitutional protections. But in wartime, different considerations applied. He still did not have the power under the Constitution to abolish slavery by decree. But as commander in chief of the nation's armed forces, he had military powers under the Constitution to free slaves in rebel states "as a fit and necessary war measure for suppressing said rebellion." This meant that the four slaveholding border states in the Union, as well as the retaken parts of Tennessee and a few other areas, were exempted from the measure.

Many observers then and since have wished for a more resounding document, something comparable to the Declaration of Independence, that would have marked the end of slavery dramatically. But such criticisms miss the point of Lincoln's statesmanship. Yes, it can justifiably be claimed that Lincoln, though often soaring in his rhetoric, tended to be careful in his actions. But that was because Lincoln wanted slavery abolished in what he considered to be the right way.

He was in no doubt that the Constitution's provision for slavery was inconsistent with the Declaration's insistence on the natural rights of all human beings. The remedying of that flaw would, he believed, render the Constitution more fully the instrument it was meant to be. But the law could be corrected only by the correct use of the law, not by overturning it. The Thirteenth Amendment to the Constitution would be the proper way to accomplish it.

And there is this also to be said: despite its understated and lawyerly language, the Emancipation Proclamation had a certain moral grandeur, precisely because it marked the moment that the war's purpose began to enlarge. Lincoln would soon make this point explicit in the Gettysburg Address a few months later in 1863. It was now clear that, by putting the process of emancipation into motion, Lincoln had determined that the war was going to be not only about the preservation of the Union but about something even greater.

22 · A WAR REDEFINED

Unfortunately, after Antietam, the Union's military fortunes quickly worsened. Lincoln's problems with the generals only got worse. If McClellan had been an excessively cautious leader, General Burnside turned out to be the opposite: rash and reckless. When he attacked Lee's army at Fredericksburg, he sent in waves of men conducting traditional charges, only to see them mowed down by Lee's well-entrenched units. The casualties were terrible – twelve thousand lost to Lee's five thousand. The following day, a tearful Burnside withdrew his decimated forces and limped away from Fredericksburg, soon to be replaced by General Joseph Hooker. As 1862 ended, the Union forces were discouraged, stuck in a war that had been longer and far bloodier than anyone had expected – and with no end in sight.

Hooker, an ambitious and vindictive man nicknamed "Fighting Joe," was unlikely to make things better. And he didn't. In May 1863, he encountered Lee's army in Chancellorsville, Virginia, with a force of 130,000, the largest Union force so far. And yet, despite outnumbering the Confederates at least two to one, he was badly beaten, partly by Lee's tactical brilliance and partly by his own bumbling leadership. A consolation for the Union, though, was that the Confederates paid heavily too. They lost even more of their men (thirteen thousand casualties out of sixty thousand) than they had at Antietam. Even worse, they lost the extraordinary General Stonewall Jackson, who died from accidental wounds produced by confused "friendly" fire from his own pickets in the darkness.

It is hard to exaggerate the impact of Jackson's death, and the grief elicited by it. He was arguably the most gifted and most beloved of all the Confederate generals, a deeply pious man who was also a brilliant tactician, the general whom Lee considered to be his irreplaceable "right arm." His loss was not only a military setback but a profound blow to the morale of the Confederate army and its leaders, and to the Southern public.

The immediate Union reaction to Chancellorsville, too, was one of shock and disbelief. But the Confederacy's heavy losses were beginning to have a noticeable effect. In fact, the war's decisive turning point was coming. In the first week of July 1863, the Confederacy suffered two colossal defeats, one in the West and the other in the East, that placed the Union well on the road to victory.

First there was Vicksburg. One part of the Anaconda Plan had involved gaining control of the Mississippi River. By spring 1863, that objective was nearly accomplished. New Orleans was under Union control, as was most of the river, and all that remained was the taking of the heavily fortified city of Vicksburg. General Ulysses S. Grant, who had been remarkably effective in securing the river and had won an important early victory for the Union at Shiloh in Tennessee, would take Vicksburg easily, by means of a punishing seven-week siege, on July 4. The Confederacy was now cut in two, and Texas and Arkansas were isolated and, in effect, lost.

Then came Gettysburg. Robert E. Lee had once again decided to take the offensive and invade the North, hoping to strike while Northern morale was still low in the wake of Chancellorsville and the defeats of 1862. If he could win a great victory or capture a Northern city, that might yet induce a foreign country to intervene or move enough discouraged Northerners to sue for peace.

On July 1, his invading forces encountered Union units near Gettysburg in southern Pennsylvania, and thus began a three-day battle that would be the most important of the war. The Union army under General George G. Meade had positioned itself on Cemetery Ridge, just south of the town. Repeated efforts by Lee's army, including a famously futile charge by General George Pickett's fifteen thousand infantry on July 3, failed to break his line or dislodge his army. Oddly, once again, Meade failed to follow up and crush the defeated Confederate force as it withdrew. But there could be no doubt about it – Lee had suffered a major defeat.

Four and a half months later, at the dedication of the Soldiers' National Cemetery near the Gettysburg battlefield, Lincoln delivered one of his greatest speeches. A masterpiece of reverent commemoration, the Gettysburg Address was also a crisp and memorable statement of national purpose and national identity. It sought to provide a higher meaning for a war that had grown into something far greater and far more destructive than had been imagined at its outset. Surely an ordeal so costly must, in some larger scheme, be for the sake of something very large – larger, perhaps, than the American people had yet realized.

In an address of fewer than three hundred words, Lincoln would redefine the war as, not merely a war for the preservation of the Union, but a war for the preservation of the democratic idea – "government of the people, by the people, for the people" – an idea for which America served as an example to the world. The speech reached back to the nation's beginnings and echoed the words of Hamilton and other Founders who saw in American history a larger purpose being carried out on behalf of all humankind. From its origins in 1776, it was to be a nation "dedicated to the proposition that all men are created equal," language that Lincoln took directly from the Declaration of Independence.

The current war, Lincoln said, was a time of testing for that idea. It was a time that had produced immense pain and suffering. There was no end to it yet in sight. But Lincoln urged his listeners to be inspired by the sacrifice that the fallen soldiers had already made and to resolve to finish the work those men had nobly begun, so that their sacrifice would not have been in vain. In conclusion, Lincoln quietly but firmly asserted that this work would include the commitment that he had made in the Emancipation Proclamation – that the nation would, under the providence of God, see "a new birth of freedom" emerge out of these sufferings.

Reports vary widely as to the audience's reaction to the speech that day in Gettysburg, but it soon became regarded as one of the classic speeches in the English language, one that British prime minister Winston Churchill (no mean orator himself) would years later call "the ultimate expression of the majesty of Shakespeare's language."

With Grant's victory in Vicksburg, and a third brilliant performance at Chattanooga by Grant and generals under his direction, Lincoln felt he had finally found the fighting general for whom he had so long been looking. By 1864, Lincoln had brought him to Virginia and given him command of the Union armies. Grant was tasked with formulating a grand strategy for victory.

There was nothing fancy about Grant's approach. It was a brutal plan, bruising and grinding, reflecting the outlook and tactics that had brought him success at Shiloh and Vicksburg. Wear the enemy down. Destroy his supply lines. Starve his army (and civilians, too, if necessary). Deploy massive blocks of troops to pound relentlessly at the resistance. Never retreat. If necessary, abandon your own supply lines and live off the land, eating up the enemy's crops and goods. Do not hesitate to suffer significant casualties on your own side, so long as you are moving forward and the enemy's capacity to fight was being steadily reduced and, eventually, destroyed.

Such tactics would have been unthinkable just three years earlier, when no one could have imagined how long, wasting, and destructive this war would turn out to be. They were hardly ideal tactics for the conduct of a civil war which aimed at an eventual reunification. But their ascendancy reflects another transformation being caused by this war. Just as what began as a war for the Union was turning into a war for freedom, so what began as a more conventional war of armies clashing in the fields of battle was turning into a total war.

Hence the American Civil War became a first glimpse of what war would become in the twentieth century: a clash of whole societies. In total war, the mobilization of each society's total assets – its economy, its culture, its transportation system, its way of life, its morale – became as important as strictly military tactics. Accordingly, the goal of war was not merely defeating the enemy on the battlefield. It was also a relentless process of destroying the enemy's ability and willingness to fight – and at the same time obliterating the confidence of enemy civilians in the ability of their government to protect them.

Grant was about to become one of the most eminent generals of military history, but he certainly didn't look the part. He was an unimpressive-looking man with stubble on his face and a slouched and unmilitary bearing. He was known for the cigar ashes that seemed a constant presence on the front of his sloppy uniform. There was not a hint of the great man about him. He finished in the lower half of his class at West Point and compiled a respectable record in the Mexican War, but then resigned from the army amid rumors of alcoholism. He went on to fail at almost everything else he tried in civilian life, finally ending up taking a position in his father's leather goods company in Galena, Illinois.

And then the war came and Grant was moved to seek appointment as an officer in the Union cause. The rest was history – a steady run of military successes that were essential to the eventual Union triumph. But the man behind those achievements has always remained hard to know. "Most men who saw U. S. Grant during the Civil War felt that there was something mysterious about him," wrote Civil War historian Bruce Catton. "He looked so much like a completely ordinary man, and what he did was so definitely out of the ordinary, that it seemed as if he must have profound depths that were never visible from the surface." Catton recalled that "even [General William Tecumseh] Sherman, who knew him as well as anybody did, once remarked that he did not understand Grant and did not believe Grant understood himself."

His effectiveness, though, was beyond dispute. In May 1864, he went back on the move, taking the 115,000 men of the Army of the Potomac south into eastern Virginia. There he engaged Lee's army in a series of bloody encounters, including the frightening Battle of the Wilderness on May 5–6, where the armies fought blindly through the woods, amid confusion and wildfires, with heavy casualties on both sides. But there would be no interruption of Grant's drive southward. He did not stop until he arrived at Petersburg, an important railroad center south of Richmond, where he trapped Lee's army and laid siege to it for the next nine months.

Meanwhile, General Sherman set out from Chattanooga, Tennessee, with a force of nearly one hundred thousand men, bound toward Atlanta and then across Georgia to Savannah and the Atlantic Ocean. Sherman's March, as it became known, was a textbook guide to the logic of total war, carried out by a man who understood that logic better than almost anyone else. Facing virtually no organized opposition, Sherman's army cut a swath of devastation sixty miles wide across central Georgia. Along the way, they seized food and farm animals, freed slaves, destroyed railroads and mills, and burned down homes, all acts designed to terrorize the population into submission.

In the midst of all this, the American constitutional system required that another presidential election be conducted in November 1864. Even a civil war could not suspend the electoral cycle. So the political dimension to all of these events could not be ignored. Lincoln could not take his reelection for granted – far from it. He had become a lightning rod for all of the public's dissatisfaction with a seemingly endless war. In his own Republican Party, while the majority supported him, the radical wing viewed him as insufficiently abolitionist and feared he would allow the South back into the Union on overly relaxed terms.

The Democratic Party, which here means only the Northern remnant of it, was divided. The War Democrats supported the war effort but wanted only a restoration of the Union as it had existed in 1860; they were not down for the "new birth of freedom." Others, such as the Copperhead faction, named for the poisonous snake, opposed the war and wanted to end it immediately on terms acceptable to the South. They thought of Lincoln as a tyrant, and some bordered on being pro-Confederate in their sympathies. The Democrats nominated General McClellan as the party's candidate, which was another jab at Lincoln, although it also complicated the election, because McClellan himself did not entirely endorse his own party's platform.

Despite the Democrats' divisions, though, there was the real possibility that Lincoln would not be able to prevail in the fall. In fact, in early 1864, before Grant's successful push to Petersburg and Sherman's taking of Atlanta and Savannah, Lincoln became convinced that he was indeed likely to lose the election. What a bitter pill that would have been – to see all his labors, all the blood spilled, and all the treasure spent in the war effort count for nothing.

Because Lincoln is so widely admired today, we tend to forget how unpopular he was during his time as president. Few great leaders have been more disdained or loathed or underestimated in their own day. And it wasn't just Southerners who ridiculed him. According to Lincoln's biographer David Donald, his own associates thought him dull, and addicted to telling bad jokes. The abolitionist Wendell Phillips called him a "huckster in politics" and "a first-rate second-rate man." McClellan openly mocked him as a "well-meaning baboon."

Lincoln's ordeals remind us that a hero's life is not like a Hollywood movie, in which the background music swells and all the audience smiles and applauds and leaps to its feet. In real history, the background music does not swell, the trumpets do not sound, and the critics often seem louder than the applause. The leader has to wonder whether he is acting in vain, whether the criticisms of others are in fact warranted, whether time will judge him harshly. Few great men have felt this burden more fully than Lincoln.

But that string of military victories, which also included Admiral David Farragut's dramatic naval victory at the Battle of Mobile Bay in August 1864, turned the tide, and by the time of Lincoln's reelection, there was little doubt about the war's ultimate outcome and that its end would be coming soon. Although Lincoln ran as a Republican, he ran as the National Union candidate, a name invented to attract Democrats and others in the border states who would not vote Republican. For similar reasons, he chose the War Democrat Andrew Johnson of Tennessee as his running mate. Their ticket won in a landslide.

The war was not yet done, though. In December 1864, Sherman finally arrived in Savannah and, after gathering his strength, in the new year marched north to Columbia, South Carolina, the very capital of secession, burning it and more than a dozen towns along the way. Then he headed to North Carolina, advancing relentlessly against Johnston's increasingly eroding army. Grant kept up the pressure against Lee's lines at Petersburg. A smell of Confederate defeat was in the air.

On March 4, Lincoln was inaugurated into his second term and once again gave a speech for the ages. In a relatively short but haunting text, he reflected on the larger meaning of this enormous conflict and began to lay the groundwork for the postwar settlement. We know from Lincoln's personal papers that he had been increasingly preoccupied with the question of God's will, of discerning how He had steered these events and to what end, and it seems clear that Lincoln had searched the Bible and various theological writings for answers. The results of his meditations are evident in his second inaugural address, a speech filled with biblical themes and imagery.

Lincoln did some remarkable and surprising things with the speech. Although he repeated the observation that slavery was "somehow the cause of the war," he resisted the temptation to assign precise or exclusive blame to either side. He also reminded his audience that the violent antagonists were brothers, part of the same culture. "Both read the same Bible and pray to the same God, and each invokes His aid against the other." And yet God's will was something larger than the objectives of either side. "The prayers of both could not be answered. That of neither has been answered fully. The Almighty has His own purposes."

Then Lincoln proposed a stunning image: that the war had, perhaps, been an atonement for the nation's sin and that God had given "to both North and South this terrible war as the woe due to those by whom the offense [of slavery] came," and moreover that such an act of atonement would be fully consistent with our understanding of God's justice. Indeed, he went on, drawing on Psalm 19:9,

> *If God wills that [the war] continue until all the wealth piled by the bondsman's two hundred and fifty years of unrequited toil shall be sunk, and until every drop of blood drawn with the lash shall be paid by another drawn with the sword, as was said three thousand years ago, so still it must be said "the judgments of the Lord are true and righteous altogether." (King James version)*

Yet the speech concludes in hopeful and peaceful terms: "with malice toward none, with charity for all"; such phrases pleaded for a spirit of reconciliation in the land, a spirit not of vengeance but of "bind[ing] up the nation's wounds" and "car[ing] for him who shall have borne the battle and for his widow and orphan," and the pursuit of a "just and lasting peace among ourselves and with all nations."

It is perhaps still astonishing, even today, to see those words "with malice toward none, with charity for all" uttered during the worst and most murderous war in American history. But Lincoln had never lost his clarity about the chief purpose of the war: it was not to punish all wickedness and establish a realm of perfect justice; it was first and foremost to restore the Union. Lincoln continued to believe that the preservation of the Union and Constitution was essential to the success of the liberty agenda that was on the verge of abolishing slavery. A postwar settlement dominated by malice and score settling, and lacking in the spirit of charity and forgiveness, would not ultimately succeed. The Christian virtues he was championing in his speech were not only morally right but also practically right and politically wise.

A month later, on April 3, Richmond fell to the Union forces. On April 9, after a last flurry of futile resistance, Lee faced facts and arranged to meet Grant at a brick home in the village of Appomattox Court House to surrender his army.

It was a poignant scene, dignified and restrained and sad, as when a terrible storm that has raged and blown has finally exhausted itself. The two men had known one another in the Mexican War but had not seen one another in nearly twenty years. Lee arrived first, wearing his elegant dress uniform, soon to be joined by Grant clad in a mud-spattered sack coat, his trousers tucked into his muddy boots. They showed one another a deep and respectful courtesy. Grant generously allowed Lee's officers to keep their side-arms and the men to keep their horses and take them home for the spring planting. None would be arrested or charged with treason.

Four days later, when Lee's army of twenty-eight thousand men marched in to surrender their arms and colors, General Joshua L. Chamberlain of Maine was present at the ceremony. He later wrote of his observations that day, reflecting on his soldierly respect for the men before him, each passing by and stacking his arms, men who only days before had been his mortal foes:

> *Before us in proud humiliation stood the embodiment of manhood: men whom neither toils and sufferings, nor the fact of death, nor disaster, nor hopelessness could bend from their resolve; standing before us now, thin, worn, and famished, but erect, and with eyes looking level into ours, waking memories that bound us together as no other bond; – was not such manhood to be welcomed back into a Union so tested and assured? ... On our part not a sound of trumpet more, nor roll of drum; not a cheer, nor word nor whisper of vain-glorying, nor motion of man standing again at the order, but an awed stillness rather, and breath-holding, as if it were the passing of the dead!*

Such deep sympathies, in a victory so heavily tinged with sadness and grief and death. This war was, and remains to this day, America's bloodiest conflict, having generated at least a million and a half casualties on the two sides combined – at least 620,000 deaths, maybe more, the equivalent of 6 million men in today's American population. One in four soldiers who went to war never returned home. One in thirteen returned home with one or more missing limbs. For decades to come, in every village and town in the land, one could see men bearing such scars and mutilations, a lingering reminder of the price they and others had paid.

And yet Chamberlain's words suggested that there might be room in the days and years ahead for the spirit of reconciliation for which Lincoln had called in his second inaugural address, a spirit of binding up wounds and of caring for the many afflicted and bereaved and then moving ahead, together. It was a slender hope, yet a hope worth holding, worth nurturing, worth pursuing.

But the tender promise of that moment would not last. Only two days later, on April 14, Good Friday, the world would change again, as President Lincoln would be shot and killed by an embittered pro-Confederate actor in Washington, D.C., while attending a play at Ford's Theater. That one action would greatly complicate the task of national reconciliation and would throw the postwar settlement into chaos. Like the Bible's Moses, Lincoln was denied entry into the promised land of a restored Union and the satisfaction of seeing that new birth of freedom for which he had labored so long and hard.

We can never know how well Lincoln's postwar leadership might have fared had he lived to oversee that process of national reunion. But what we do know for certain is that, in his absence, the factions he had managed to keep at bay for so long would no longer be held back by his reasonableness and constraining moderation. Winning the war had been very hard. Winning the peace was now going to be even harder.

23 · THE CHALLENGE OF RECONSTRUCTION

THE REUNION OF the nation presented overwhelming problems. First and foremost was the problem of the economic devastation that total war had wrought in the southern states. Cities like Richmond and Columbia and Charleston had been reduced to ruins, with rotting wharves and empty streets lined with bombed-out buildings. The railroad system was a shambles, factories were destroyed, and farmlands lay fallow. Property values had collapsed; Confederate bonds and other paper assets had been rendered worthless. No investment money was flowing into the region to help restart failed businesses or create new ones.

Nor was there means to restart southern agriculture, since the system of slave labor on which the South had relied for much of its agricultural production was gone, and the wealth of planters gone with it. Cotton, tobacco, sugar, rice, hemp: all were but shadows of their former status and would require decades to recover, if they did at all.

Most heartbreaking of all was the unsettled state of freed slaves. They found themselves wandering in a strange and unfriendly new world, without money, without land, and with few of the skills required to participate in a free economy. They had a freedom in name that fell very far short of being freedom in fact.

Their prior condition had been, as Lincoln had said, one of the principal causes of the war. But now it was as if their present plight was forgotten, even by abolitionists. "He was free from the old plantation," wrote Frederick Douglass of the freedman, "but he had nothing but the dusty road under his feet." The Freedmen's Bureau, established in March 1865, just before the war's conclusion, was a well-intentioned but insufficient attempt to use the War Department, in cooperation with private organizations, such as the American Missionary Association, to address some of these massive problems.

By contrast to the humiliated South, in many respects the North had prospered from the war. With the troublesome planters out of the political picture entirely for four years, the business community had been able to dominate the Congress and promote the passage of legislation favorable to their interests. Long-standing objectives of the Republican Party, such as protective tariffs (the Morrill Tariff) and free land for western settlers (the Homestead Act), were easily realized. The National Banking Act created a uniform system of banking and currency, and naturalization requirements for immigrants were eased. In addition, the much-debated location for the first transcontinental railroad was settled in the North's favor; the north central line would run from Omaha, Nebraska, to Oakland, California, with the golden "last spike" driven with a silver hammer at Promontory Summit, Utah, in May 1869.

The inequality of the two sections, which proved a persistent problem well into the twentieth century, helped give rise to a view that the war had actually been a "second American Revolution," a social upheaval in which businessmen, laborers, and farmers of the North and West drove the planting aristocracy of the South out of power. There was some truth in this. Particulars aside, it is a view that captures the fact that the America of the post–Civil War era was dramatically changed in many respects.

There were numerous issues to wrestle with in thinking through the reunification of the nation. What would a just settlement look like? How should the Southern rebels be punished, for example? Should the leaders be imprisoned, charged with treason, put to death? What about their followers, including the Confederate officers whom Grant had allowed to return home after Appomattox with their sidearms and horses, or the Confederate infantry who had fought for them?

And what about the demolished southern economy? Given that the southern economy had depended so heavily on slavery, the economy of the South would have to be restructured. But how? Who would do it? Who would pay for it? How could the freed slaves be equipped for life as free individuals, with the ability to participate in this economy? Would they be given their own land? Would they be treated as full equals in every respect?

There were two opposite views among victorious Northerners about how to proceed in reunifying the nation. Some wanted to bring the South back with as few complications and penalties as possible, maintaining as much of the former structures as possible. Others felt that anything less than a severe punishment of the South, accompanied by a complete social and political transformation, would not be enough and would represent a betrayal of the war effort. It was a fairly stark choice, both as a philosophical issue and as a practical matter. Were the returning Southerners to be treated as restored states or as conquered provinces?

Lincoln had thought about the subject a great deal and had concluded that, since secession itself was illegal, the Confederate states had never actually left the Union; and since they had never left the Union, it made the most sense to demand only a very low standard of loyalty be met as a condition for restoration to full membership in the Union. As early as December 1863, he had formulated a plan whereby pardons would be offered to those who agreed to swear an oath of loyalty to the Union and Constitution and who pledged to accept the abolition of slavery. Then, under Lincoln's plan, a state would be readmitted if 10 percent of the voters in that state had taken the loyalty oath. High officials and ranking military officers would be excluded from the pardon, but otherwise, the offer was quite sweeping.

It was a very generous plan, indeed, and much too lenient in the eyes of many of Lincoln's fellow Republicans in Congress. They were convinced of the need for a thorough remaking of southern society, one that would take apart the old southern class system and substitute something radically new in its place. They also were convinced that the Congress, and not the president, had principal authority over such decisions in the first place. To these ends, they proposed and passed the Wade–Davis Bill, which required not 10 percent but a *majority* of voters to swear that they had never been loyal to the Confederacy.

Lincoln pocket-vetoed the bill, meaning that he refused to sign it and allowed it to expire unapproved. The Radical Republicans who supported the measure were outraged and accused Lincoln of exceeding his presidential authority. In fact, the question of which branch of government was authorized to preside over the readmission of states was not easily answered from the text of the Constitution. There was no precedent for this.

Lincoln's final statement on the subject came in his last public address, on April 11, just two days after Lee's surrender at Appomattox. The subject at hand was whether Louisiana should be accepted back as a reconstructed state, based on a new constitution that abolished slavery and otherwise was sufficient to meet his standards, though not enough to please the Radical Republicans. A letter writer had complained to him that Lincoln was unclear about whether the seceding states were in or out of the Union. Lincoln waved the question away as a "pernicious abstraction" and then went on to explain his view in what might be called a masterpiece of constructive evasion:

We all agree that the seceded States, so called, are out of their proper relation with the Union; and that the sole object of the government, civil and military, in regard to those States is to again get them into that proper practical relation. I believe it is not only possible, but in fact, easier to do this, without deciding, or even considering, whether these States have ever been out of the Union, than with it. Finding themselves safely at home, it would be utterly immaterial whether they had ever been abroad. Let us all join in doing the acts necessary to restoring the proper practical relations between these States and the Union; and each forever after, innocently indulge his own opinion whether, in doing the acts, he brought the States from without, *into the Union, or only gave them proper assistance, they never having been out of it.*

The key to success, it seemed, lay in not defining things too precisely.

And so matters stood three days later, on the day of Lincoln's assassination. That morning, during a meeting with his cabinet, Lincoln spoke, hauntingly: "I hope there will be no persecution, no bloody work, after the war is over.... Enough lives have been sacrificed. We must extinguish our resentment if we expect harmony and union. There has been too much of a desire on the part of some of our very good friends to be masters, to interfere with and dictate to those states, to treat the people not as fellow citizens; there is too little respect for their rights. I do not sympathize in these feelings."

That night at Ford's Theatre, during a performance of *Our American Cousin*, at around 10:00 P.M., his assassin, John Wilkes Booth, entered the president's box with a pistol in his hand. After firing a fatal shot into Lincoln's head at close range, he leaped onto the stage and shouted "Sic semper tyrannis!" the Latin motto which means "Thus always to tyrants." Lincoln himself would become the first victim of the bloody work whose coming he had so greatly feared.

Never in history has a true-believing fanatic committed a crime that did more damage to his own cause. The South could not have had a better friend than Lincoln in the hard years that lay ahead. True, the man from Illinois might or might not have been able to prevail in implementing his plans for a generous, mild peace between North and South. He was already facing stiff opposition to his 10 Percent Plan in his own party, and that might have intensified. But he also was experiencing a surge of popularity in the wake of the Union's final victory, and it is possible that he could have summoned the political support to overcome such opposition. It is also possible that his plan would have proved unworkable, even with him doing the implementing. We shall never know.

As it was, however, the brutal murder of Lincoln made the

national mood toward the South turn darker, harder, more angry, more vengeful. It did not help matters that, in Andrew Johnson, who now rose to the presidential office, the country would have a president with little of Lincoln's political intelligence and even less of his eloquence and generosity.

Johnson had been added to the ticket in 1864 as a unity candidate from the border state of Tennessee. He was a War Democrat who opposed secession but had none of Lincoln's enthusiasm for a "new birth of freedom." Although he had served as a congressman, governor, and senator from Tennessee, his origins were just as humble as Lincoln's. He grew up among the poor whites and small farmers of North Carolina and eastern Tennessee, and he closely identified with them, while deeply resenting the wealthy planters, whom he held responsible for the calamity that had enveloped the South. These sympathies and resentments were the driving forces in his political career. He rose politically in Tennessee by championing the cause of poor whites in their conflicts with the wealthy planters. The Republicans in Congress embraced him for that reason, and anticipated being able to work well with him, perhaps more easily than with their own Lincoln. Surely he would want to punish the South, they thought, especially after the events at Ford's Theatre. Surely he would embrace the cause of social transformation in the South.

But they deceived themselves. They heard him protest against secession and wealth and assumed that meant he was one of them. They failed to see that Johnson's hostility toward Southern aristocrats was due, not to sympathy for the poor and powerless, but to resentment of his social superiors. He fully shared all of his white constituents' deepest prejudices against black people and had little or no objection to the institution of slavery. That was not what the Civil War was about, not for him. And he most emphatically did not share his Republican colleagues' desire to see the entire South humiliated, only the rich planters.

Johnson was the wrong man for the job in other ways. The times called for a leader confident enough to take the long view and not let the slings and arrows of everyday political debates upset him. But that was not Andrew Johnson. He was a mass of insecurities and hatreds, with a grudge-holding, narrow, and petty mind and a wounded and fearful soul. Historian Eric McKitrick described him as an outsider, deeply convinced that all the organized forces of society were against him. If Lincoln provided a living illustration of the fact that a common man of humble background can rise to the heights of American politics, Johnson became a living illustration of the fact that not all common men can manage that rise successfully, no matter how ambitious they may be.

Johnson's problems began early on. In May 1865, he put forward a Reconstruction plan that was only slightly more demanding than Lincoln's. By the time the Congress reconvened in December, all eleven of the ex-Confederate states had met the criteria to be incorporated as functioning states of the Union. They had organized governments, ratified the Thirteenth Amendment to the Constitution (abolishing slavery), and elected senators and representatives. All that remained was for the Congress to accept and seat them.

But this was not going to happen. For one thing, none of the Southern states had extended voting rights to blacks as part of their new constitutions. And for another thing, there were former Confederate leaders, including generals, colonels, and cabinet members among the new congressional delegations. Alexander Stephens, the former vice president of the Confederacy, was elected U.S. senator from Georgia, even though he was still in prison awaiting trial for treason!

Furthermore, many legislatures were adopting "black codes" that regulated and restricted the rights and behavior of former slaves. Such codes varied from place to place but could include prohibitions on landownership and allow long-term labor contracts that were hardly distinguishable from slavery.

The Republicans were seriously divided between moderates

and radicals. But those divisions did not extend to any willingness to tolerate such negative developments, which seemed to reflect an attitude of southern defiance. Indeed, their perception of such defiance, along with still-fresh memories of Lincoln's assassination, tended to unite Republicans behind the Radical position. The Republicans in Congress briskly rejected Johnson's approach to the readmission of states, refused to seat the new crop of senators and congressmen, and instead created a Joint Committee on Reconstruction to study the question. The committee highlighted evidence of the mistreatment of blacks under the new state regimes and concluded that Congress, not the president, was the appropriate authority to determine how the states could be restored. Up to this point, the process of reconstruction had been guided by the president. The committee was mapping out a different future.

In the meantime, in early 1866, Johnson made things much worse for himself with two inflammatory vetoes. First, he vetoed a bill to extend the life of the Freedman's Bureau, arguing that it had been a wartime measure but that because the war was over, the extension of the bureau into peacetime would be unconstitutional. Although his veto was controversial, it was narrowly sustained.

Then he vetoed the Civil Rights Act, an act designed precisely to counter the black codes and other forms of grossly unequal treatment being restored in the postwar South, and that featured language establishing that "all persons born in the United States" were entitled to "full and equal benefit of all laws."

Johnson justified his veto by saying that the act went beyond the proper scope of federal powers and would lead to racial disharmony and conflict. But this time, his veto was overridden – the first time in American history that a major piece of legislation had been enacted into law over the veto of a president. Shortly thereafter, a new Freedman's Bureau bill was also passed over Johnson's veto.

These events marked the beginning of a new era, both for Reconstruction and for presidential–congressional relations. And it marked the beginning of the end for Johnson's effectiveness as president.

24 · HOPES GAINED AND LOST

To clarify the intentions behind the 1866 Civil Rights Act, and remove any doubt about its constitutionality, the Joint Committee recommended the creation of a new constitutional amendment, the Fourteenth, which was passed in June 1866 and declared ratified by the states by July 1868. The amendment was much more far-reaching than the Civil Rights Act, however, and more complex. It represented the first attempt to give constitutional definition to the concept of citizenship.

First of all, it declared that all persons born or naturalized in the United States were citizens. (A "naturalized" citizen was an immigrant or noncitizen who had acquired citizenship status through a legal process.) It obligated the states to respect and uphold the rights of citizens, assured citizens they could not be denied "equal protection of the laws," and assured them that their rights could not be taken away without "due process of law." That portion of the amendment was significant because it extended to the individual states the requirement that they respect the rights of citizens, in just the way that the federal government was required to do within its own sphere. Thus the Fourteenth Amendment began a process, culminating in the 1920s, called *incorporation*, which refers to the extension of the protections of the Bill of Rights to the state constitutions and governments.

These provisions, all coming from the first section of the five-section amendment, had more long-term significance than other parts of the amendment. But those other parts had great, even explosive, significance in the immediate term. In particular, the second section was aimed directly at the southern states' refusal to grant voting rights to their black citizens. By the terms of the amendment, if a state kept any eligible person from voting, it would be penalized by having its representation in Congress and the Electoral College reduced accordingly.

As the fall elections of 1866 drew near, an angry and frustrated President Andrew Johnson decided to go for broke. He decided to make a "swing around the circle" of northeastern and midwestern cities, denouncing his Radical opponents as traitors and making opposition to the Fourteenth Amendment and support for his lenient approach to Reconstruction his central theme, along with support for his preferred candidates, most of them Democrats, in the upcoming congressional elections.

This was risky even under the best of circumstances. For one thing, in those days, presidents didn't do political campaigning, and there were concerns that his doing so would seem undignified. At first the tour went extremely well, as Johnson stuck to his script and resisted the temptation to go off topic. In Cleveland, however, he lost his composure, had a shouting contest with a heckler, and made other unwise remarks that were picked up and printed in the newspapers. During later appearances in other cities, matters only got worse, and by the end, in many places, spectators' loud shouts drowned his efforts to speak.

Thus the swing around the circle ended up being a complete failure. Johnson himself later acknowledged that it did him more harm than good. In the congressional elections that fall, the Republicans swept to landslide victories, leaving both houses of Congress with huge, veto-proof Republican majorities. Johnson would never again have any control over the agenda moving forward. The wresting of control over Reconstruction by the Congress was now mostly complete, and a new stage of Reconstruction was about to begin. With this change came a major shift in the structure of constitutional governance, since almost everything to come next would be imposed by the Congress over the strong objections of the president and the Supreme Court. Never before had Congress reigned so fully over both; never before had any one branch of the federal government so completely dominated the other two.

In early 1867, the Congress passed three Reconstruction Acts that in effect treated the South as a conquered province. It abolished the state governments for the time being, divided the territory into five military districts, and placed it under military occupation. The requirements for readmission to the Union were also made much more strict; the ex-Confederate states now had to ratify the Fourteenth Amendment and incorporate into their state constitutions measures that would ensure that all adult males, irrespective of race, would have the right to vote.

In addition, Congress passed something called the Tenure of Office Act, which prohibited the president from removing a federal official from office without the consent of the Senate. The measure was probably unconstitutional, but its purpose was completely understandable in political terms: the Radicals wanted to make sure that Johnson could not fire the Radicals in his cabinet, such as the secretary of war, Edwin Stanton, who oversaw the administration of the military governments in the South. Johnson took the bait, however, and went ahead and fired Stanton anyway. The House of Representatives responded to that act by impeaching Johnson on February 24, 1868, and seeking to remove him from office.

The stage was set for one of the great dramas of congressional history. Under Article 1, section 3 of the Constitution, impeached presidents undergo trial in the Senate with the chief justice of the Supreme Court presiding, and with a two-thirds vote of that body required for conviction. Johnson's trial lasted for three months of high drama and intrigue, playing to a packed gallery of onlookers. In the end, when the vote was taken, the margin was razor thin owing to the defection of Republicans who feared the precedent established by Johnson's removal. The result came down dramatically to a single, unexpected vote against impeachment from Republican senator Edmund Ross of Kansas.

Johnson survived, but only by the barest margin, and his effectiveness as president was now at an end. He would be passed over for the Democratic nomination for president in 1868, and, as if to add to the repudiation, Edmund Ross would lose his bid for reelection to the Senate two years later. Bitter and combative to the end, Johnson made his last act as president one that would outrage his enemies: he issued a pardon to former Confederacy president Jefferson Davis. But that ineffectual gesture changed nothing. The Radical tide continued to sweep in and swamp all before it.

At their own 1868 convention, the Republicans chose as their presidential candidate General Ulysses S. Grant, a certified war hero who had no political experience. He was viewed as a sure vote getter, in the way that Whig military heroes like Zachary Taylor had been. But Grant won the presidency by a surprisingly modest margin in the popular vote (3 million to 2.7 million), a fact that gave added impetus to the swift passage of the Fifteenth Amendment, which was meant to protect ex-slaves' right to vote. The 1868 electoral results showed the Republicans how important it would be to protect the votes of newly empowered African Americans if the Republicans were to continue to triumph.

With the ratification of the Fifteenth Amendment, the Radicals had succeeded in getting their way in the South. Or had they? All the southern states were under Republican governments and had not only succeeded in getting blacks the right to vote but, in some cases, had actually elected blacks to public office. Hence the rather misleading term "Black Republican" Reconstruction that is sometimes applied to this period.

But in fact the actual government of those states was nearly always in the hands of whites, many of them northerners who had come to the region out of a wide variety of motives, ranging from saintly idealism to selfish opportunism. These outsiders were unaffectionately labeled "carpetbaggers" by white southerners who resented their intrusion. White southerners who had chosen to cooperate with Republican governments earned the even more sneering name of "scalawags."

Leaving aside the names, though, how effective were these governments? More generally, how effective was the Reconstruction program of the Radical Republicans? The record is mixed, as are the opinions of historians. But it is fair to say, first, that there were many accomplishments, in areas such as civil rights, internal improvements, hospital building, and the creation of public school systems. There also were failures, evidenced both in the spread of corrupt practices in the awarding of state contracts and in the lack of honest and efficient political leadership. To be fair, though, this was a problem that was appearing all over the nation, and particularly in the big cities of the North, just as much as in the South. Under the circumstances, spectacular successes were too much to hope for; even a minor success was a major achievement.

What were conditions like for the freed slaves? They had not received the "forty acres and a mule" that they had hoped for at the war's end, which meant that for the foreseeable future, they would not have their own land and would still have to work for white landowners. And since the landowners needed the ex-slaves' labor, eventually systems like sharecropping and the crop-lien system emerged that made this possible. In both systems, farmers received seed, tools, and necessities from their landlords, in exchange for which the farmers would agree in advance to turn over a percentage (usually one-third to one-half) of what they produced. Because the rest of the crop was often committed to paying off debts, the resulting system often resembled slavery in a great many ways, with no escape from the web of obligations.

In addition, although much progress was made in improving many aspects of African American community life – marital and family stability, education, and independent churches all improved markedly – and creating unprecedented access to the mainstream political system, there was also visible and rising racial hostility toward them. By the time Grant had assumed the presidency, there were increasing instances of antiblack sentiment and activity in the South, including the founding in 1867 of the Ku Klux Klan and similar organizations whose members roamed the countryside, hidden behind masks and robes, issuing threats, scattering rumors, and occasionally perpetrating acts of savage violence and terrifying destruction. All their measures were designed to intimidate the black population, and also any white Republicans who took the "wrong" side of things.

At Grant's insistence, Congress passed three Enforcement Acts in 1870–71, designed to combat these groups and their attacks and protect the voting rights of blacks in the South. But the acts suffered from weak and inconsistent enforcement, and the groups they were designed to inhibit did not stay inhibited. In fact, they only seemed to gather strength. Under this growing pressure, blacks began to stay home on election days, and little by little their political influence in their respective Southern states waned away; Democrats resumed control.

The difference can be illustrated in a single stark example. In overwhelmingly black Yazoo County, Mississippi, in 1873, Republicans cast 2,449 votes, Democrats 638; only two years later, the Democrats received 4,049 votes, and Republicans received 7. The terror campaign had succeeded. In state after state, white southern counterrevolutionaries, who became known as "redeemers," were taking control, a process that was complete by 1877. It was an astonishingly fast reversal of what had seemed a profound change.

Where was the North in all this? It seems that the great reformist tide that had begun decades before with the antislavery movement, carried the cause of emancipation to its completion, and then swept Andrew Johnson out of power was now rapidly ebbing away. Zeal was out; weariness and distraction seemed to be setting in – weariness in that after four years of horrifying war and nearly a decade of anxious and conflict-ridden "peace," and decades before that of agitation over the slavery question, the problems of the South were beginning to seem impossible to solve, distraction in that other matters were now occupying their attention. There were the distractions of settling a new continent and absorbing and exploiting the massive assets of a newly continent-spanning nation. This included such concerns as westward exploration and expansion, railroad construction, industrial development, Indian wars, and, above all, the eager pursuit of prosperity in the rapidly expanding postwar economy.

Other forces were also at work. As memories of the war itself began to fade, older loyalties began to reassert themselves. Yes, Virginia had been the North's bitter enemy of late. But had it not been the case that George Washington, and Thomas Jefferson, were Virginians, and national heroes of the highest order? That Andrew Jackson was a southerner? That Lincoln himself was a southerner by birth? The mystic chords of memory of which Lincoln spoke in his first inaugural address – the chords whose sounding would express the harmony of a reunited country – had not been silenced forever by war. A desire for a greater measure of national reunification welled up, a desire that was hard to deny – even if it meant closing one's eyes to the incomplete social revolution of the South.

The final blow to Reconstruction came with the presidential election of 1876, which turned out to be one of the most corrupt and controversial presidential elections in American history. The Republicans nominated Rutherford B. Hayes, governor of Ohio, a former Congressman and a wounded Civil War veteran. The Democrats nominated Samuel J. Tilden, a wealthy corporate lawyer and reform-minded governor of New York who had actively opposed corrupt government in New York City and Albany.

The campaign itself made it obvious how thoroughly the tide of reform zeal had exhausted itself. Neither candidate supported the Radical agenda; both favored a more lenient approach to the South. Indeed, they disagreed on very few substantive issues, which meant that the campaign was mainly devoted to slurs and irrelevancies. The Democrats mocked the Republicans for their corruption. The Republicans "waved the bloody shirt" at Democrats, taunting them with the charge that the Democrats had been the party of secession and the cause of the Civil War.

The electoral results were inconclusive. While Tilden won the popular vote by 250,000 votes, he was one vote short of a majority in the Electoral College, with several southern states still contested.

There was a blizzard of claims and counterclaims by the two parties. In the end, the Congress, which was itself divided, set up an electoral commission to decide the outcome. Through various intrigues, Hayes was able to carry the committee vote 8–7, along party lines. Democrats were outraged at this result and threatened to use the tool of a filibuster to block Hayes, or to march on Washington to force the inauguration of Tilden.

It never came to that, as cooler heads prevailed. An agreement, which became known as the Compromise of 1877, was worked out between the Republicans and a group of southern Democrats who were willing to defect, for a price. The deal was relatively simple. The Republicans would promise that Hayes, if made president, would withdraw the last federal troops from the South, allow the last two Republican state governments (Louisiana and South Carolina) to collapse, and commit to the construction of a southern transcontinental railroad. In return, the Democrats would drop their opposition to Hayes and agree to accept the three Reconstruction Amendments to the Constitution (the Thirteenth, Fourteenth, and Fifteenth). It was a bargain all parties were willing to accept.

With the Compromise of 1877, the era of Reconstruction came to an end. It is hard not to see it as having been a failure. Consider these words of a former slave named Henry Adams, who became a soldier in the U.S. Army and a landowner and community leader in Shreveport, Louisiana, but who reacted with undisguised dismay to the Compromise:

> *In 1877 we lost all hopes.... We found ourselves in such condition that we looked around and we seed [sic] that there was no way on earth, it seemed, that we could better our condition there, and we discussed that thoroughly in our organization along in May.*
>
> *We said that the whole South – every State in the South – had got into the hands of the very men that held us slaves – from one thing to another and we thought that the men that held us slaves was*

holding the reins of government over our heads in every respect almost, even the constable up to the governor. We felt we had almost as well be slaves under these men.

There had indeed been a moment, a glimmer of hope for a better, different future. Over the next three decades, though, the protection of black civil rights in the South was crushed by the white "redeemer" governments' rise to power. The progress that had been made was soon forgotten.

And in a strange way, the earliest (and generally pro-southern) chroniclers of Reconstruction, such as the followers of Columbia historian William A. Dunning, who saw Reconstruction as an unmitigated disaster, were of a similar disposition – even if they came to that disposition from an entirely different direction, one that was critical of Radical Reconstruction for attempting too much, rather than achieving too little. In their eyes, too, Reconstruction had been a failure.

Might these bleak testimonies, though, have understated the difficulty of the task, and the worthiness of the positive achievements brought about in those turbulent years – even if only as essential groundwork laid for better and more enduring solutions in a day yet to come? That is possible too.

It is hard to find the right balance in such matters, and each generation is likely to reckon the balance differently. The improvement of a culture is extremely long and difficult work. Even the best intentions can produce unexpected and unwanted consequences. Hence the wisdom in Lincoln's poignant comments at his last cabinet meeting. He would never have approved of Johnson's callousness or of the postwar southern attitude of defiance. But he also understood, better than the Radicals of his own party, that the humiliation of the white South was not going to produce the results he had sought either – indeed, that it might produce entirely opposite results.

But amid all the arguments and counterarguments, one should not lose sight of the concrete benchmarks of achievement – the

Thirteenth, Fourteenth, and Fifteen Amendments to the Constitution, changes in the structure of the nation's fundamental laws ensuring that, the next time around, the language of our fundamental law could be on freedom's side, just as Lincoln had wanted it to be.

One thing is for certain. The deeply unsatisfying episode of Reconstruction left far too much work undone and a great many wounds unhealed. That work and that healing would remain tasks for generations to come.

ACKNOWLEDGMENTS

THE PRINCIPAL ACKNOWLEDGMENTS that I have expressed in the original edition of *Land of Hope* remain the relevant ones here. I won't repeat all of them, much as I am tempted to, but will say only that my debt to my colleagues and friends at the University of Oklahoma remains great, as do my debts piled up through the years to my teachers, colleagues, friends, and family, especially the wonderful person to whom the book is dedicated, my wife, Julie.

In addition, I want to mention that I have relocated to Hillsdale College as of August 2021, where I gratefully accepted an appointment as the Victor Davis Hanson Chair of Classical History and Western Civilization. Hillsdale has a deep and comprehensive commitment to the improvement of instruction in American history and government at all levels, and more generally to the restoration of civic education, a subject that we have badly neglected, to our considerable detriment. It is an honor to be associated with such an extraordinary institution and with its admirable mission.

Finally, I'd like to thank several individuals who gave me invaluable assistance in the preparation of the text, particularly in finding a comfortable pitch for the reading level. Molly Kopf, a relatively new teacher with a veteran's eye for detail, scoured the prose in search of the author's occasional lapses into verbal grandiosity. So, too, did Holly Monteith, whose editing and proofreading were superb, as always. Don't blame either of them if we didn't catch everything. And last, but not least, I must mention the whole Encounter Books staff, from Roger Kimball and Sam Schneider on, and particularly

Amanda DeMatto, some of the most amazingly smart and patient people I know. Not only are they wonderfully competent but they are always a joy and a privilege to work with.

INDEX